In the Meantime

In the Meantime

Living in Light of the Ascension

Gordon T. Smith

CASCADE *Books* • Eugene, Oregon

IN THE MEANTIME
Living in Light of the Ascension

Copyright © 2025 Gordon T. Smith. All rights reserved. Except for brief quotations in critical publications or reviews, no part of this book may be reproduced in any manner without prior written permission from the publisher. Write: Permissions, Wipf and Stock Publishers, 199 W. 8th Ave., Suite 3, Eugene, OR 97401.

Cascade Books
An Imprint of Wipf and Stock Publishers
199 W. 8th Ave., Suite 3
Eugene, OR 97401

www.wipfandstock.com

PAPERBACK ISBN: 978-1-6667-8373-5
HARDCOVER ISBN: 978-1-6667-8374-2
EBOOK ISBN: 978-1-6667-8375-9

Cataloguing-in-Publication data:

Names: Smith, Gordon T., author.

Title: In the meantime : living in light of the ascension / Gordon T. Smith.

Description: Eugene, OR: Cascade Books, 2025 | Includes bibliographical references and index.

Identifiers: ISBN 978-1-6667-8373-5 (paperback) | ISBN 978-1-6667-8374-2 (hardcover) | ISBN 978-1-6667-8375-9 (ebook)

Subjects: LCSH: Jesus Christ—Ascension. | Christian spirituality. | Cosmology.

Classification: BT500 S65 2025 (paperback) | BT500 (ebook)

VERSION NUMBER 08/18/25

for joella

Contents

Introduction | ix

1. From the Empty Tomb to the Mount of Olives | 1
2. The Six Redemptive Acts of God in Christ Jesus | 16
3. The Character of Christian Worship | 31
4. Personal and Solitary Prayer | 49
5. Christian Mission in the Meantime | 69
6. Vocation and Work in the Meantime | 85
7. Praying the Psalms | 100

Bibliography | 111
Scripture Index | 113
Author Index | 115
Hymn and Song Index | 117
Subject Index | 119

Introduction

WE LIVE AND PRAY and work in the meantime: between the ascension of Christ Jesus, and the final consummation when the kingdom will be fulfilled. Theologians speak of the "already" and the "not yet." The already: Christ has come; Christ is establishing his kingdom on this earth. Christ is ascended. This is gospel—good news. And then also there is the "not yet": the fullness of the kingdom has not yet appeared. It is yet to come. Christ is ascended and bringing about his kingdom but the kingdom has not yet been fully revealed or fulfilled. In the meantime, we live and worship and work. *How* do we do this? How do we live and work with integrity and with resilience, specifically a resilient hopefulness in the meantime?

Jesus came announcing that the kingdom of God was at hand (Mark 1:15). But then at the conclusion of the Gospel narratives the disciples are asking: Is this the time? Will the kingdom be fulfilled now? And the answer is the ambiguous "it is not for you to know" and that the Father will establish the kingdom in God's timing. We live and work, then, in the *meantime*.

Everything we do is informed by the confidence we have that the incarnate, crucified, risen Lord is ascended and has gifted the world with the Spirit and will one day appear and make all things well. In that sequence from incarnation to consummation, everything pivots on the ascension. Thus, the opening verses of Colossians 3:

> So if you have been raised with Christ, seek the things that are above, where Christ is, seated at the right hand of God. Set your minds on the things that are above, not on the things that are on earth, for you have died, and your life is hidden with Christ in God. When Christ who is your life is revealed, then you also will be revealed with him in glory. (Col 3:1–4)

Introduction

This book is an invitation to, in the words of verse 2: "set your minds on things that are above." Why? Precisely because of what we read in verse 1: that our lives are now found in Christ, who is seated at the right hand of God.

Then also, consider the call from the New Testament book that gives so much attention to the ascension, Hebrews:

> Therefore, since we are surrounded by so great a cloud of witnesses, let us also lay aside every weight and the sin that clings so closely, and let us run with perseverance the race that is set before us, looking to Jesus, the pioneer and perfecter of faith, who for the sake of the joy that was set before him endured the cross, disregarding its shame, and has taken his seat at the right hand of the throne of God. Consider him who endured such hostility against himself from sinners, so that you may not grow weary in your souls or lose heart. (Heb 12:1–3)

The Hebrews text is the essential complement to the words of Colossians, a reminder to set our minds on things above. We see clearly that this is not a mere intellectual exercise: rather it is heart, soul, mind, and strength that are all aligned with the ascended Christ Jesus.

The genius of living "in the meantime"—between the already and the not yet—is specifically an inner orientation that necessarily has to be and very specifically must be on Christ: not the mere idea of Jesus, not a theological concept, but a person, the living and ascended Christ.

To live and work in the meantime, with integrity, strength, joy, and hopeful resilience, is to be in intentional and dynamic fellowship with the ascended Christ Jesus. There is an immediacy in all of this: a profound awareness of the presence of Christ in our lives, in our world, and in the church. And further, this awareness needs to be cultivated. It is learned; it is practiced; it is an awareness that requires constant tending. If we are to, in the words of the book of Hebrews, persevere and run the race that is before us, even in the face of hostility, we need to focus on the risen and ascended Christ. Again, it is an encounter with a person (not a mere idea); it is not mere religion, but a dynamic, living, and generative—yes, even *redemptive*—engagement with the living and ruling Christ Jesus.

All of this calls for a specific focus: to celebrate the ascension, to be aware of what it means and then to align our hearts and minds accordingly. When we get it—that the ascension matters and makes all the difference—it leads to an *intentionality* in our worship and prayer as well as a very specific approach to vocation, work, and ministry. And we ask: what is Jesus

Introduction

doing—specifically, what is Jesus doing today? When it comes to mission and our work, this the heart of the matter because living in the meantime, in light of the ascension, is living and acting and working in response to what Jesus is doing today.

Recovering a Dynamic Awareness of the Ascension

We ask: What does the ascension mean to the life and witness of the Christian community? And, how does the reality of the ascension make a difference to the Christian community? What does it mean to cultivate a posture or disposition, an alignment of life and work and worship with the ascension?

In response to these questions we first consider what happened and what it means. We tell the story—the sequence of events that led to the ascension proper. But then and crucially, we ask the *meaning* question. We ask: Why does it matter? And what difference did it make and does it make today? In what follows we will have a theology or doctrine of the ascension spelled out. But more specifically, we need to consider what the ascension means for Christian spirituality—specifically for what it means to be the church as we live intentionally in light of the ascension. To this end, there will be two primary reference points: worship and work. We begin with what the ascension means for our worship and our individual and personal prayer. But then we shift and consider our work in the world and our participation in the mission of God through and in the ascended Lord Jesus Christ. Worship and work; and we will speak to the interplay between them.

So first, in chapter 1, we tell the story: just as we do for the nativity scene each Christmas and then later into the church calendar we tell the story of both Good Friday and Easter Sunday. In like manner we tell the story of the ascension, from the empty tomb to the Mount of Olives. From there we move to the *meaning* and significance of the ascension—specifically to what it means to speak of Christ as both high priest and as Lord of the cosmos and the church. Then we look in subsequent chapters to the character of our worship and our prayers and to our participation in the purposes of God—the mission of God—in the church and in the world.

Most of all, what we come to see and know is that in and through the ascension the benevolence of God is known and experienced. We learn what it means to live in the love of God—or better what it means to be rooted and grounded in love and what it means to have "the power to

Introduction

comprehend, with all the saints, what is the breadth and length and height and depth" of the love of God in Christ so that we are filled with the fullness of God (Eph 3:17–18).

1

From the Empty Tomb to the Mount of Olives

JESUS MADE IT CLEAR to his disciples that the ascension was an integral part of his program. It was not an afterthought or merely a tag-on to what had already happened. From the beginning Christ became incarnate, went to the cross, and rose again so that he would be glorified—that is, in the language of the New Testament, that he would be seated at the right hand of the Father, positioned in the place of executive authority. From the beginning, this was the anticipated outcome. Jesus came proclaiming the kingdom (Mark 1:14–15) and anticipating when all authority would be given to him (Matt 28:17). The way to this end was through birth, death, and resurrection. But the ascension was the intended outcome.

In John 14 Jesus explains to his disciples that he will go away and that this is for their own good. Because then he will be the way to the Father so that where he is they also will be. And then, still in the Gospel of John, we have the encounter with Mary Magdalene near the empty tomb, where Jesus advises her not to touch him because he has not yet returned to the Father. Despite the full, embodied resurrection, Jesus still had to ascend into heaven.

We read in the Gospels and the book of Acts that following the resurrection, Jesus spent forty days with the disciples. It was largely a time of teaching—with the primary emphasis being the nature of the kingdom of God (Acts 1:3). And yet what is also noteworthy is that Peter with Cornelius also speaks of this as a time when Jesus ate and drank with the disciples (Acts 10:41).

This is clearly temporary—a liminal or transition time in which it is confirmed again and again for the disciples that Jesus was risen from the dead and thus remained fully *embodied*. We have the emphasis at the end of Luke where Jesus is pressing them to see his wounded hands and his feet, insisting he is no ghost but the risen and embodied Jesus they have had known all those years (Luke 24:39). He taught them, he ate with them; he confirmed the reality of his resurrection.

And yet, there is a growing sense that more was yet to come. Sure enough, after forty days he led them across the valley to Bethany (in the book of Luke) or the Mount of Olives (in the book of Acts), which is where Bethany is located. The kingdom of God was on their minds. As they came to the Mount of Olives, the disciples were asking "Lord, is this the time when you will restore the kingdom to Israel?" (Acts 1:6). In response, Jesus reminded them that it was not for them to know the specifics, but he assured them that the time would come when the kingdom would be fulfilled.

Then we read that he was "lifted up"—taken out of their sight. Craig Keener observes that in Acts 1 Luke is clearly describing this event through the lens of the experience of Elijah (2 Kgs 2)—that is, Luke intimates that the ascension of Jesus is of the same type as Elijah's. The first readers of the Gospel accounts would have recognized the significance of this. They would have known of Elisha observing the ascension of Elijah and that, in like fashion, the first disciples witnessed the ascension of Jesus.[1]

The event is described by Luke with four key references.[2] First, Jesus is taken up into a cloud, which, Keener notes, is an allusion to glory. The ascension is the glorification of the Son. Second, there are angels who provide the interpretation of the event, much as they did for the resurrection (Luke 24:4–7). In this case, the angels confirm the meaning of what the disciples had just witnessed. The reference to heaven speaks of the place or home of God. This is now where Jesus is. And then we have, fourthly, the assurance that Jesus will return, in the same way as he left.

Jesus is now "in heaven"—meaning not so much "up there," but rather that Jesus stepped into—or, better, was *taken into*—a different sphere of reality. He was drawn into another realm of existence.

---

1. Keener, *Acts*, 719.
2. On this, following Keener, *Acts*, 725ff.

From the Empty Tomb to the Mount of Olives

We may wonder about the cosmology; what happened and how did it happen? But in our understandable speculation, we cannot miss the main point: Jesus is now "at the right hand" of the Father. The first disciples and then subsequently the church are witnesses to the ascended Christ and to the reign of Christ in the world and in the cosmos.[3]

Jesus Christ as High Priest

So that is what happened. But what does it mean and what is Christ Jesus doing today? The twofold response is that Christ Jesus is now both high priest and cosmic Lord. For the role of high priest, we turn to the book of Hebrews. The ascension is the great focal point and central message of Hebrews. It is often noted that if we neglect the book of Hebrews, we likely will not have an appreciation of the central importance of the ascension in the redemptive work of God. The book opens with these words:

> Long ago God spoke to our ancestors in many and various ways by the prophets, but in these last days he has spoken to us by a Son, whom he appointed heir of all things, through whom he also created the worlds. He is the reflection of God's glory and the exact imprint of God's very being, and he sustains all things by his powerful word. When he had made purification for sins, he sat down at the right hand of the Majesty on high, having become as much superior to angels as the name he has inherited is more excellent than theirs. (Heb 1:1–4)

Kwame Bediako, one of the leading African theologians of the last century, makes an important observation. The book of Hebrews—which, he insists, is OUR epistle (upper case is his emphasis—meaning *the* epistle of the African church).[4] Hebrews presents Christ as the high priest, yes, but very specifically as high priest in line of Melchizedek rather than the order of Aaron. Bediako finds this tremendously significant, for it signals that we are transcending the priesthood of a particular people—that is, perhaps, the Hebrew people—and as is stressed in Hebrews 7 and 8, the priesthood of Melchizedek speaks of "the priesthood, mediation and hence salvation that Jesus Christ brings to all people everywhere,"[5] transcending clan, family, tribe, and nation. As Bediako puts it, "The quality of the achievement

---

3. Keener, *Acts*, 721.
4. Bediako, *Jesus in Africa*, 27.
5. Bediako, *Jesus in Africa*, 28.

and ministry of Jesus Christ for and on behalf of all people, together with who he is, reveal his absolute supremacy."[6]

In John 14 Jesus speaks of himself as the "way" to the Father. And more, that to know Jesus is to know the Father. As such, Christ Jesus is the focus of the worship of the church. He is glorified to this end: that we might be brought into fellowship with the Father and with the Triune God.

Therefore, the Christian community is a worshipping people. And in worship and prayer, Christ is both the object and means by which we come into the presence of the Triune God. What is Christ doing today? He is receiving the adoration and worship of the Christian community. Christ is our high priest through whom our worship and prayers reach the Father.

The worship of the church now, at this time, is a foretaste of the worship that will be offered at the consummation, when every knee will bow and every tongue will confess that Jesus is Lord. But in the meantime, the church does not wait but even now offers unbounded praise and adoration to the Son.

It is helpful to think of two dynamics that happen in our worship. First, Christ is the object of our praise. And then, second, we worship in and *through* Christ. Thus the liturgy of the church begins with thanks and praise and adoration to the one who sits on the throne. But, we also offer "the prayers of the people." In the words of Hebrews 4:14–16, we offer these prayers with confidence knowing that Christ hears us and identifies with us and will be the means by which we know grace in our time of need. Thus, the Christian faith and Christian worship is decidedly and intentionally Christocentric: Christ is the focus of our worship and our prayers.

In our worship, we encounter the risen and ascended Lord. We behold him and this encounter is redemptive. In the work and ministry of Christian discipleship, this is the most powerful and grace-filled way by which a person is *transformed* into the image of Christ: through the actual encounter with the ascended Lord. While this experience is mediated by the Spirit through the gift of Pentecost, the focus remains set on Christ. We look to Jesus. In and through Christ we are brought into the glorious fellowship of the Triune God.

So first, in what follows, we must speak of worship as the intentional act of the Christian community by which we bring glory and praise to Christ Jesus and, further, by which, *through* Christ, we pray with and through our high priest. However we speak of worship or liturgy or our common

---

6. Bediako, *Jesus in Africa*, 28.

prayers, it all comes down to this: we are brought into the presence of the ascended Lord. Then also in our personal prayers, the individual practice of contemplative prayer, here too we are drawn into the presence of the ascended Lord and we learn to know and live in the love of God in Christ. Shared worship; individual prayer. Both are essential and essential *together* in the formation of the Christian believer. And it naturally follows that we ask: What is the character of the worship that brings us into fellowship with the Triune God through Christ Jesus? What does it mean that our worship is not merely talking about Jesus but meeting Christ in a real-time encounter? And what do our daily and personal prayers look like and feel like if and as we, in relational and solitary space, are in the presence of Christ?

The Ascended Jesus Christ Is Now Lord of the Cosmos and Lord of the Church

The focus of the book of Hebrews is on Christ as high priest. The perspective that complements this is the witness of the apostle Paul to the cosmic lordship of Christ. The apostle affirms the extraordinary wonder that now, by virtue of the ascension, all things come under the authority of the ascended Jesus:

> God put this power to work in Christ when he raised him from the dead and seated him at his right hand in the heavenly places, far above all rule and authority and power and dominion, and above every name that is named, not only in this age but also in the age to come. And he has put all things under his feet and has made him the head over all things for the church, which is his body, the fullness of him who fills all in all. (Eph 1:20–23)

It is this vision that anchors the epistles to the Ephesians and the Colossians. The whole of the magisterial Letter to the Ephesians hinges on the declaration that Christ is now seated at the right hand of the Father and in the place of authority—"all power and dominion, and above every name that is named"—and as such the lord of the church. But more, as Colossians emphasizes, Christ is now "head over every ruler and authority" (Col 2:10). And as head of the church and Lord of creation, he is, we read, "pleased to reconcile to himself all things" (Eph 1:15–23).[7]

---

7. See also Colossians 1:18–20.

As the one to whom all authority has been given (Matt 28:18) he then commissions his disciples to be participants in the mission of God in the world. Through his disciples he would build his church and through them witness to the reign of God in the world. Thus, with the ascension, Christ assumes two roles. First, that of high priest and intercessor, mediator between earth and heaven, between humanity and the Father, as we see so clearly in the book of Hebrews. And second, that of Lord: Christ is now Lord of the church and of the world, inaugurating his reign of peace and justice. As Peter declares on the Day of Pentecost, the one who was crucified has now been made both Lord and Messiah (Acts 2:36). And he has invited us, called us, to do "good works" very precisely as the reflection of what God in Christ is doing in the world.

This is why we speak of both worship and work: from worship we turn from liturgy to our labor in the world, from *encounter* with the ascended Christ we turn to *engagement* with our world. This dual response will inform our reflections here: what does the ascension mean for the call to and the character of our *worship* of the ascended Christ? And, what does the ascension mean for our work in the world through which and by which we *witness* to the reign of Christ?

There is something in all of this that cannot be missed—something fundamental to our identity and purpose as those who worship and serve the ascended Lord Jesus Christ. The presence, power, and purpose of Christ ascended is universal and cosmic in scope. On the one hand, Christ Jesus is, by virtue of the ascension, Lord of all. And as cosmic Lord, Christ Jesus is reconciling all things to the Father. The vision of the Lordship of Christ is all-encompassing, comprehensive, cosmic. Jesus Christ is not merely or only or even primarily my personal Lord and Savior; it is personal, but it is so much more: it is *cosmic*.

And that cosmic vision also emerges when we speak of Christ through the other dimension, as high priest. The Book of Common Prayer—the BCP—has had profound influence in the worship of the Church of England and Anglican communities around the world. But the BCP is potentially a devotional guide for all Christians. Early in the worship of the BCP we have the "Gloria in Excelsis." This is typically referenced simply as the "Gloria," no doubt due to the opening word and line, "Glory to God." The whole of the Gloria reads:

> Glory to God in the highest,
> and peace to his people on earth.
> Lord God, heavenly King,
> almighty God and Father,
> we worship you, we give you thanks,
> we praise you for your glory.
> Lord Jesus Christ, only Son of the Father,
> Lord God, Lamb of God,
> you take away the sin of the world:
> have mercy on us;
> you are seated at the right hand of the Father:
> receive our prayer.
> For you alone are the Holy One,
> you alone are the Lord,
> you alone are the Most High, Jesus Christ,
> with the Holy Spirit,
> in the glory of God the Father.
> Amen.

On the one hand, this is a classic example of worship that opens with a full affirmation of the ascension. Christ Jesus is the holy one who is seated at the right hand of the Father. The ascension is, then, front and center in our worship. And in celebrating and affirming the ascension there is a line that cuts us to the quick: "Lamb of God, you take away the sin of the world . . . have mercy on us."

The Gloria is a testimony to the benevolence of God and the wideness of God's mercy. Even more: the line "you take away the sin of the world" is a reminder that the ascension speaks not merely to something that has been transacted for me and my sins and thus for the sake of my salvation. The high priest, Christ Jesus and ascended Lord, is at the right hand of the Father and is the very one who takes away the sin of the entire world.

Thus we see the powerful interplay between Christ as high priest and Christ as cosmic Lord. The one who takes away the sin of the world is one and the same as the Christ who is now reconciling all things to the Father.

And so, we enter into the presence of the Father through our high priest; this is the essence of our worship. And we participate with the cosmic Lord in the mission of God in the world; this is the meaning of both the mission of the church and also for each of us, our personal sense of purpose and vocation.

There is actually a psalm where all of this comes together. It is of note that Psalm 110 is the most quoted or referenced psalm in the New

Testament. But this should come as no surprise since in this Psalm we testify to Christ Jesus as both high priest and cosmic Lord. It is a psalm of David that celebrates the Messiah who will indeed rule on the throne and fulfill the priesthood of the order of Melchizedek.

The Question of Identity: Finding Home, Hidden in Christ

But then, we also need to highlight that with the ascension we find our true identity—our home with the Father and the Son and the Spirit. We are now citizens of heaven. In the language of 1 Peter, we are exiles and aliens in this world. But our primary loyalty and identity—our true home—is with Christ in heaven. Contrary to the popular song that suggests that "we are just a'passin' thru," we *are* residents of this world; we are fully present to this world. And yet, our identity and loyalty and the focus of our hearts is on the ascended Christ.

This is what it means to live and worship and work in the meantime with integrity, courage, purpose, and joy, with our hearts and minds drawn to and aligned with the presence of the ascended Christ. We can, in the words of John 15:4, abide in him as he abides in us. Or, as the apostle Paul puts it in Colossians, we can set our hearts and minds on Christ—not as a mere thought experiment or as a principle or fact of our lives. Rather, we can know what it means that our lives are "hidden with Christ" in God (Col 3:3). Christ is in us even as we are in Christ; the encounter is personal, existential, and immediate.

To get some sense of what this signifies—what it means to us—one window of insight again comes to us through the Psalms. The Psalms consistently speak of an extraordinary dynamic between heaven and earth—an intimate connection. Thus Psalm 46: "God is our refuge and strength . . ." (Ps 46:1), and the God of Jacob is our refuge (Ps 46:7). We know the grace of the Twenty-Third Psalm—the immediacy of the one who is our shepherd, who restores the soul that is feeling the threat and uncertainty of what the psalmist speaks of as walking through the "darkest valley," without fear, for we know that God is with us.

We are where Jesus is, in the presence of the Father. Through the ascension, we are brought into the holy of holies. Here we find rest for our weary souls. Here we find our true identity; we are, finally, at home. We have been brought into the company of the Triune God.

From the Empty Tomb to the Mount of Olives

Remember the words from the hymn "Come Thou Fount," which includes the line which we sing: "prone to wander Lord I feel it, prone to leave the God I love; take my heart, take and seal it, seal it for the courts above." That is precisely the grace we seek: to be sealed for the courts of heaven, where Christ is seated at the right hand of the Father.

But Wait: There Is More; Onwards to Pentecost

How is this even possible? How can we even begin to speak of how through our worship we enter into fellowship with the Triune God—that we are *there*, in the heavenly place, with Christ? How can we have the audacity to suggest that in our prayers and in our worship we are in fellowship with the high priest of heaven and with him and through his prayers brought into the holy place?

And how can we pretend to even begin to be participants in the mission of Christ to the world, the work of cultivating the life of the church and bringing reconciliation to all things? Can we truly witness to the reign of Christ and in so doing participate in the kingdom purposes of God in the world?

The answer, of course, is captured expectantly in one word: "wait." At the ascension, Jesus speaks of his departure and the coming kingdom of God but then he urges his disciples to *wait* (Acts 1:4). He is leaving but there is one who is yet to come (as he also makes clear in John 14). The full meaning and experience of the ascension is only possible through the grace of the Holy Spirit who is yet to come. Thus they are to wait.

It is by the Spirit that we bring glory and praise and our prayers to our high priest. It is by the Spirit that we are in Christ and participants with Christ in his work in the world. All worship—each aspect and element of Christian worship—is graced by the Spirit. And, further, it is the Spirit that calls, anoints, and empowers us for the work we are called to do with and for the ascended Christ.

Thus, a true ascension theology and spirituality is deeply informed by the understanding and experience of the Spirit. Ascension Day is and must be linked very closely to Pentecost. The only ascended Christ we know is the Christ who is present to us through the grace of the Spirit. Even so, the only Spirit we know is the one who brings us into the worship of the Son and who equips and empowers us to work for and with the Son.

In the Meantime

The Witness of Charles Wesley

Few have witnessed to the ascension as intensely and with such grace as the hymn writer Charles Wesley, brother to John, who was both an astute and articulate theologian as well as a hymn writer.

Consider "Arise, My Soul, Arise," a Wesley classic. Here Wesley anticipates the language of Matthew Bridges's "Crown Him with Many Crowns" with the remarkable line where Bridges has us sing: "Crown him the Lord of love, Behold His hands and side, Those wounds yet visible above, In Beauty glorified . . ." That was a line or perspective I originally attributed to Bridges, and yet the same image—"those wounds yet visible above"—emerges a century earlier in Wesley, where in his hymn we sing: "Five bleeding wounds He bears, Received on Calvary, They pour effectual prayers, They strongly speak for me . . . ." Then comes the grand conclusion, classic Wesley: "With confidence I now draw nigh, With confidence I now draw nigh, and Father, Abba, Father, cry."

Consider also Wesley's "I Know That My Redeemer Lives." The opening line is a straightforward reference to the ascended Christ who is our high priest: "I know that my Redeemer lives, And ever prays for me." But then think especially of Wesley's "Rejoice, the Lord is King," where we sing:

> 1 Rejoice the Lord is King;
> Your Lord and King adore!
> Rejoice, give thanks and sing,
> And triumph evermore.
> Lift up your heart,
> Lift up your voice!
> Rejoice, again I say, rejoice!
> 2 Jesus, the Saviour, reigns,
> The God of truth and love;
> When he had purged our stains,
> He took his seat above;
> Lift up your heart,
> Lift up your voice,
> Rejoice, again I say, rejoice!
> 3 His kingdom cannot fall,
> He rules o'er earth and heav'n;
> The keys of death and hell
> Are to our Jesus giv'n:
> Lift up your heart,
> Lift up your voice,

From the Empty Tomb to the Mount of Olives

> Rejoice, again I say, rejoice!
> Rejoice in glorious hope
> Our Lord and Judge shall come
> To take his servants up
> To their eternal home
> Lift up your heart,
> Lift up your voice,
> Rejoice, again I say, rejoice!

Notice the sequence of ascension themes that Wesley includes in this hymn; it is a full theology of the ascension in four verses.

Verse 1 opens with unbounded praise to the ascended Christ. Verse 2 echoes the wording of the opening verses of the book of Hebrews—"having made purification for sin . . ." Verse 3 highlights the themes of Ephesians and Colossians, and then verse 4 affirms our confidence in the future. And, not to be missed, is the recurring call "lift up your heart."

Matters of the Heart

That recurring line in Wesley—Lift up your heart!—merits our attention. Wesley has us sing it again and again, and rightly so. It signals something of note: worship as a matter of the heart.

Where and how do we meet the ascended Christ? Where and how do we encounter Jesus when in this life—in the meantime, between the ascension and the consummation—if we do not see him or hear him or touch him directly? If the literal face-to-face encounter with the reigning Christ is yet to come—at the consummation of the kingdom—how do we hear and know and encounter Christ *now*, in the meantime?

When we speak of seeing Christ with the eyes of faith, or, when we speak of the need to attend to the voice of Jesus—for "my sheep hear my voice" (John 10)—where and how does this happen? What is the point of encounter with the ascended Christ?

Here is where the ancient witness consistently brings us back to the interior life. In one of his sermons for the Feast of the Ascension, St. Augustine urges his hearers to ascend with Christ as they let their hearts be lifted up.[8] And then later he insists to his hearers that they "turn their attention to your own heart" if they want to see and know God in Christ, for, in the language of the Beatitudes, it is the clean of heart that will see God (Matt

---

8. Sermon 261, #1.

5:8). What we learn is that the encounter with Christ is an interior one. And this necessarily means that we are going to use the language of the heart—the interior experience of affect, desire, longing, emotion, and inner consciousness.

Central to shared Christian worship is the call known as the *sursum corda*: "lift up your hearts." When we speak of personal and solitary prayer, we lean into the wisdom of the mystical tradition, including St. Teresa of Avila, who speaks, in Spanish, of the *moradas*—the interior *dwelling places* of God, often translated as the interior castle. What all mystical theologians remind us of, all the way back to Augustine, is that the essence of spiritual maturity and strength is the ordering of the affections and that wise Christians attend, therefore, to matters of the heart.

Our encounter with the ascended Christ is not ultimately about right thinking. Faith is not in essence a rational exercise—saying that "I have faith because I believe certain things to be true" or, I am "saved" because I believe this or that or the other. Our faith in the ascended Christ is not ultimately based on what in my university days was known of as "evidence that demands a verdict."[9] Rather, we must speak to the interior life and to matters of the heart.

The challenge or problem, one might say, is that the inverse is also not true or helpful. Christians tend to slip into either one-sided rationalism or its polar opposite, expressive sentimentalism. The orientation or assumption seems to be that Christian faith is a matter of good feelings. For the first, our faith rests on those things we know to be true; for the second, it rests on the *felt* awareness of the presence of the Spirit. Neither, in the end, is true to Christian experience or, most significantly, true to our encounter with the ascended one.

Intellect matters; what we know to be true matters. We do confess our faith with conviction about those things we hold to be true. While the essence of our faith is not reason or rationality, our response is not a rejection of intellect or scholarship or clear and critical thinking. Part of the danger with subjective, expressive sentimentalism is the lack of accountability. With it we become our own authority: we trust our own heart rather than genuinely recognizing our capacity for self-deception and the need for an external locus of authority. The vulnerability we have if we downplay or dismiss the life of intellect and reason is that the Jesus we presume to

---

9. In my university years we were all reading Josh McDowell's *Evidence that Demands a Verdict*; we were convinced that a rational apologetic would win the world.

worship and know is nothing but the Jesus who is the projection of our subjective selves. We so urgently need to turn and encounter the Jesus who is witnessed to through the ancient text of Scripture and who then in turn is affirmed by the ancient creeds and historic witness of the church through the centuries. Yes, we can and must affirm the priority of the interior life—matters of the heart. But the only truly interior and authentic spiritual life is one where we are in fellowship with an authoritative community that is immersed in the sacred text—Scripture—and which then in turn affirms the witness of the ancient creeds.

Thus, religious leaders will often bemoan what they speak of as a cultural shift from an external to an internal locus of authority—speaking of this as a cultural phenomenon and one of the challenges of our day to an authentic Christian faith. And they are right that this is a problem if the net result is that each person becomes their own final authority in their own eyes. But the solution is not authoritarian rationalistic fundamentalism. Rather, the hope for the church is to cultivate authentic interior experience—wherein each person knows personally and truly the love of God in Christ for them—and know this while in fellowship with a faith community where the Scriptures are preached and where the community itself stands aligned with the Christian intellectual and spiritual tradition and does not itself presume to be the final authority.

But then, with that caveat—that the life of the mind is both essential and foundational—we can and must affirm the priority of the interior life—matters of the heart. Recognizing this leads to a critical affirmation—something central to the call to wisdom in the book of Proverbs. The wisdom literature of the Old Testament understandably affirms the need for teaching and knowledge which, in turn, leads to wisdom. But in the midst of this call to teaching and knowledge and wisdom we read: "keep your heart with all vigilance, for from it flow the springs of life" (Prov 4:23).

This explains a fascinating aside in St. Augustine's sermons on the ascension when suddenly—it seems out of nowhere—he says: "Be quick to forgive the sins committed against you. Let no one nourish anger against another lest he obstruct his own prayer to God."[10]

Knowing what we know about the priority of the interior life and the place of the affections, this aside actually makes complete sense: we cannot encounter the ascended Lord if our hearts are consumed with anger or fear or any form of desolation. Thus we have the call of 1 Timothy 2 that we are

---

10. Sermon 261, #9.

not to lift holy hands in worship while angry or in argument (1 Tim 2:8) and the parallel exhortation in the book of James, that we are to be slow to anger and quick to listen and in worship receive the word of God with meekness (Jas 1:19–20). We therefore guard our hearts. We seek the ordering of the affections.

It is in worship and in personal prayer that we hear afresh the words of the ascended Christ: Peace I leave with you; my peace I give to you . . . do not let your hearts be troubled (John 14:27). And in this we are reminded that the defining dynamic of the Christian life is precisely that we live and work in this troubled and fragmented world as women and men of whom it can be said that their hearts are not "troubled." Rather, we live and work as those of whom it can be said that they know the peace that transcends all understanding (Phil 4:7), which guards our hearts and our minds in Christ Jesus.

And thus many of us lean into the exquisite reference in the hymn "Come Thou Fount," the line that sings: "tune my heart to sing thy grace." I revel in the language of "tune my heart"—echoing the perspective of spiritual masters who throughout the history of the church have urged us to seek the ordering of our affections, the alignment of our interior lives with the reality of the ascended Christ.

For this alignment to be the tenor and texture of our lives, we need to be worshippers and pray-ers. If we are to be fully present to our world but as citizens of heaven, if we are to be in but not of this world, there are two fundamental practices that are the means by which this dual identity is sustained: common worship, with the people of God (to be discussed in chapter 3); and personal and solitary contemplative prayer (to be explored in chapter 4).

And throughout, we can keep in mind the words of the immortal hymn:

> Praise to the Lord, the Almighty the King of Creation.
> O my soul praise him, for he is thy health and salvation;
> All ye who hear, brothers and sisters draw near
> Praise him in glad adoration.[11]

The second verse of this hymn opens with "Praise to the Lord, who o'er all things so wondrously reigneth." The third verse opens with "Praise to the Lord, who doth prosper thy work and defend thee; surely his goodness and mercy here daily attend thee."

---

11. "Praise to the Lord, the Almighty," Joachim Neander; English translation Catherine Winkworth.

From the Empty Tomb to the Mount of Olives

And the point is that this is happening now, in real time. We draw near, we know the grace of goodness and mercy that "daily" attends us. In the midst of the warp and woof, the weal and woe, the joys and sorrows of our *daily* experience, we know this consolation—formed in our hearts through the encounter with the risen and ascended Lord. In worship and prayer we have cultivated within us an interior disposition, an orientation of the heart. This is therefore our recurring theme—the *sursum corda*: lift up your hearts. And it is from this posture that we participate in the mission and purposes of God in the world. It is from this interior disposition of heart that we encounter and live in the benevolence of God manifested to us in the ascension.

2

The Six Redemptive Acts of God in Christ Jesus

It is helpful to think of the salvation of God in Christ as a sequence of six acts: incarnation, cross, resurrection, ascension, Pentecost, and the consummation in the last days. When we confess our faith through the words of the Nicene Creed, our affirmation rehearses this very sequence. We declare:

> **Incarnation**: "the Lord Jesus Christ . . . for us . . . and for our salvation, came down from heaven, and was incarnate by the Holy Spirit of the Virgin Mary, and was made human . . ."
>
> **Cross and Crucifixion**: "and was crucified also for us under Pontius Pilate . . . . He suffered and was buried . . ."
>
> **Resurrection**: "and on the third day He rose again, according to the Scriptures . . ."
>
> **Ascension**: "and ascended into heaven and sits on the right hand of the Father . . ."
>
> **Consummation**: "and He shall come again in glory to judge both the living and the dead: whose kingdom shall have no end."

And what is assumed is then confessed in the next article of the creed: that the Spirit was given on the day of Pentecost: "the Holy Spirit, the Lord and Giver of Life, who proceeds from the Father."

The Six Redemptive Acts of God in Christ Jesus

This sequence—the salvation of God in Christ Jesus—is, of course, a single act of redemption. And yet, each of these aspects matters; each is an integral part of the whole and each has redemptive significance in its own right. Not insignificant is that we see the same sequence in the Apostles' Creed: "born of the Virgin Mary, suffered under Pontius Pilate, was crucified, dead and buried . . . the third day he rose again from the dead. He ascended into heaven and sits at the right hand of God the Father Almighty; from there he will come to judge the living and the dead."

Taken together, these six acts speak of God acting in Christ to heal and restore humanity and the whole of the created order. Each act matters; each is integral to the purposes of God. We cannot leave any one of these out when we speak of the salvation of God in Christ Jesus.

This sequence is then reflected in the church calendar. Each year we relive these great acts, from the first Sunday of Advent, as we enter into the mystery of the incarnation, through to Christ the King Sunday, the grand finale to the church year. This is the meaning of the church calendar: celebrating, but more, *living* into the reality in our worship and the ministry of the Word that in Christ the salvation of God is fulfilled. From Advent to Christmas through Epiphany and Lent towards Holy Week, year in and year out, the church affirms the extraordinary sequence of Christ's birth, life, death, resurrection, and ascension.

The church rightly takes a day to affirm the significance of the cross—what we speak of on Good Friday—to affirm again and live in the reality of the death of Christ and its significance for our lives. And then on Easter Sunday we affirm afresh that death was and is defeated.

Thus, incarnation, cross, resurrection, ascension, Pentecost, consummation each have their significant marker in the church calendar. However, while all six are indispensable, while all six are integral to the purposes of God in Christ, there is no doubt that some get more air time than others. And, conversely, some may get very little attention. Thus, for example, the ascension, celebrated on Ascension Day and Ascension Sunday, tends to be hardly noticed by many if not most Christians. Many church traditions make no reference at all to the ascension. Ironically, in many church contexts, Mothers' Day gets more profile than Ascension Sunday.

But the question needs to be asked. Should we not give the ascension its due, along with the other great acts of God in Christ? But more, could it be that the ascension (with Pentecost) is actually the high point in this sequence and thus potentially the defining *focus* in the worship of the church? Might it be that in fact the whole of this sequence coalesces in the affirmation of the ascension and that in a very real sense, the ascension gives meaning to each of the others?

Consider each of the acts of God in Christ again, but this time through the lens of the ascension. Note how we can demonstrate that each only has meaning and significance to the Christian community because of and in light of the ascension.

The Incarnation and the Ascension

The birth of the Christ Child is *gospel*, good news that can and must be celebrated. But when we put it in perspective, we see that the incarnation was to a very particular end: the ascension. The baby was born to be king. This is aptly captured in another of Charles' Wesley's hymns, the Advent song "Come, Thou Long Expected Jesus," which includes this verse:

> Born thy people to deliver;
> Born a child, and yet a King;
> Born to reign in us forever;
> Now thy gracious kingdom bring.

What Wesley does in an Advent hymn is point ahead to the very thing that we celebrate on Christmas Day: the child is born to be king. Herod understood this and the magi from the east understood this: the later chose to worship him; the former was threatened and sought to kill him.

Mary, the mother of our Lord, understood this. Her magisterial Magnificat is an ode to the one who would be the ascended Lord and King. In other words, Christmas only makes sense in light of the ascension; Christmas and the ascension are necessarily twinned; they each only have meaning in light of the other.

But more, there is another vital and essential link between the incarnation and the ascension. In the current social and religious climate there is a palpable longing for heightened experience—as often as not expressed as a longing for an experience of the Spirit. However legitimate such a desire or longing might be, the danger is that in a Spirit-centered piety and worship we lose a sense of the centrality of Christ in our worship and personal experience—very specifically the incarnate and oh-so-very embodied Christ Jesus. Seen rightly, the ascension does not leave the incarnation behind. Rather the incarnation is fulfilled and completed in the ascension. The ascension is very

The Six Redemptive Acts of God in Christ Jesus

specifically the ascension of the in-the-flesh, fully human Jesus. It is not just any Jesus whom we worship: it is the incarnate, crucified, and risen Lord, of course; it is a fully *embodied* Christ Jesus who is seated on the throne. Thus we worship the one who in his transformed *physicality* is present to the church, in his full humanity.

This will be the theological basis for the approach to personal prayer and contemplation—to see and appreciate the high continuity between the oh so very human Jesus revealed in the Gospels and the one to whom we pray in our worship and our personal prayers. We thus intentionally turn from a spiritualized Jesus—which is nothing but a projection of our own desires rather than a submission to the Christ Jesus who is the revelation of the Father to us.

Further, what we find is that Christian traditions that take the incarnation seriously recognize that in the holy meal—the Lord's Supper—Christ is physically present to the church and to each Christian: he gives his very embodied self to us (see the witness of John 6).

The Cross and the Ascension

From the incarnation, we move to the cross. Even as the incarnation is not the end but a means to an end, the same could be said of the cross. Much is missed when the cross is equated with the whole of the salvation of God in Christ—when we do not appreciate that the meaning of the cross is fulfilled in the ascension.

In the end our focus is not the cross, but the crucified one who is now ascended. We worship the one who, in the words of the book of Revelation, is the lamb who "is seated on the throne" (Rev 7:10). This is not just any lamb but very specifically the lamb that was slain or, as Jacque Ellul put it, "the immolated lamb."[1] Perhaps this is precisely why in the book of Hebrews the two—cross and ascension—are consistently twinned. We see this in Hebrews 1:3b: "when he had made purification for sins, he sat down at the right hand of the Majesty on high." But then this sequence of cross and ascension is repeated numerous times throughout the book of Hebrews. The testimony of this New Testament book is that the cross is taken up and integral to the *current* work of Christ Jesus. We read in Hebrews 9, building on the older witness to the temple sacrificial system, that Jesus now is the

---

1. Ellul, *Apocalypse*, 117.

high priest who enters into the holy of holies not with the blood of goats and calves, but with his own blood (Heb 9:12).

As will be stressed in an upcoming chapter, our worship is not an encounter with the cross: it is, rather, a real-time encounter with the *crucified* one. And while the cross is a fitting symbol of our faith, our worship brings us into the presence of the slain lamb, the one who sits on the throne of the universe. Our lives are lived not only in gratitude for what Jesus has done for us (on the cross) but in dynamic fellowship with him as our crucified, risen, and ascended Lord.

Typically Catholic Christians have the crucifix front and center in their church facilities and worship. Evangelical Christians protest that Christ is risen and so they make much of what they speak of as an "empty cross." But to both I say: Is there a way to capture the reality that the crucified one now rules and brings healing and wholeness to the whole of creation as the one who was crucified and who yet bears those wounds and is for all eternity the immolated lamb?

Thus our focus in worship and work is not so much the cross as the person who was crucified and still bears the marks of the cross. In our vocations, we are joint heirs with him in his sufferings (Rom 8:17). This is a *current* reality in our lives—an ever-present dynamic, that in life, worship, and work we are in fellowship with the crucified one. I can appreciate why some Christians are inclined to venerate the cross, but in the end the one who captures our hearts and minds and attention is the Lamb who sits on the throne.

In all of this, while the cross is past, it is now fulfilled in the ascension such that our focus is not so much on the past but on the current reality of the lamb on the throne. The danger, perhaps, is that if the cross is the focal point of our faith and spiritual experience we all too frequently conclude that "salvation" is atonement; they become one and the same. Our salvation undoubtedly includes and assumes the atonement gained at the cross—our sins are forgiven, shame is gone. This is good news, of course—and a vital dimension of our knowledge of the salvation of God in Christ. And yet, the salvation of God is not merely forgiveness: it is restoration, healing, and reconciliation. It is making all things well; it is the reign of justice and wholeness and shalom. It is the reconciliation of all things to the Creator. The means to this end is the cross. For sure! The salvation of God cannot happen without the cross. But we necessarily move, as we find in the book of Hebrews, from the cross to the ascension. In our worship, we venerate

The Six Redemptive Acts of God in Christ Jesus

and praise not so much the cross as the one who now reigns in glory as the crucified one. We move from forgiveness to healing. Christ not only died that we might know forgiveness; he died and rose and ascended so that we might know the restoration and reconciliation of all things—our healing and the healing of the whole of the creation.

The Resurrection and the Ascension

On Easter Sunday we celebrate the triumph over death and the grave. Rightly so. However, the resurrection itself is but the first movement, stage one, we might say. The triumph of God is not so much the resurrection as the risen one is now ascended. The risen one is now the one who reigns. When it is said that "every Sunday is Easter Sunday," perhaps we could actually see that it may be more accurate to say that every Sunday is Ascension Day. We encounter the risen Christ, not so much as he appeared to Mary in the garden or to the two on the road to Emmaus, but as the triumphant and ascended Lord. It is not as if each Sunday we imagine ourselves coming to the empty tomb; rather, each Sunday we do *actually* encounter the ascended Lord.

As Douglas Farrow puts it so well, for many the ascension "is quickly assimilated to the resurrection . . . commonly passed over as a redundant marker on the road to Pentecost."[2] But perhaps the reverse should be the case: that the resurrection is incorporated into the ascension: that the resurrection sets up and is *fulfilled* in the ascension. Nowhere is this more evident than in the book of Hebrews, where the resurrection is taken for granted, one might say, as the cross and the ascension are twinned—as noted in the reference above from Hebrews 1:3. The resurrection is not even mentioned; it does not need to be because it is assumed with the reference to the ascension. Or elsewhere, where the resurrection is mentioned, it is actually in view of the ascension, such as in Ephesians 1:15, where with reference to Christ we read that God "raised him from the dead and seated him at his right hand in the heavenly places."

Again, as Farrow notes, when the resurrection and the ascension are conflated, we lose a sense of the goal of salvation history.[3] It is not, in the end, merely about the triumph over death; it is not in the end merely about resurrection. Rather the goal of history—salvation history—is the triumph

2. Farrow, *Ascension and Ecclesia*, 9.
3. Farrow, *Ascension and Ecclesia*, 28.

of God over all the forces of darkness and evil and, ultimately the restoration and healing of the cosmos—the reconciliation of *all things* to the Creator. To this end, death needed to be defeated; but it was (only, dare we say?) one step towards the ultimate triumph of God in Christ—namely, the ascension.[4] John Calvin stresses this point, noting that though Jesus' resurrection was a vindication; it was with his ascension that his reign began.[5]

So we, of course, celebrate Easter Sunday and affirm unequivocally that Christ is risen, risen indeed, and that the forces of death have been defeated. This is good news—very good news. And yet, it is a precursor to what is yet to come—an essential marker along the way to the ultimate triumph of God in Christ, when the risen Lord meets his disciples on the Mount of Olives and declares that all authority in heaven and earth have been assigned to him. He is the sovereign one and as Lord of the cosmos and Lord of the church will bring about mission of God in the church and in the world. We can even say that the whole point of the resurrection was that the risen Lord would now be seated at the right hand of the Father. Christ Jesus became flesh and lived among us; was crucified and risen; all to this end, the triumph of the ascension. Everything in the life, work, and ministry of Jesus was and is to this end.

Following the resurrection, Jesus spent forty days meeting with and eating with his disciples and teaching them about the reign of God—the kingdom—all in anticipation of the day when this will all be fulfilled. Yes, we celebrate the resurrection, but we do so as part of an essential sequence of great acts of God in Christ, and we see in the inertia, or the momentum, a distinct movement: from the incarnation to the cross and the triumph of Easter, to this end: the ascension.

---

4. Within a typical Anglican order for the words of institution for the Lord's Table, the congregation is invited to affirm their faith with the words, *Christ has Died, Christ is Risen, Christ will come again*. This is good, of course, but as friend and colleague Darrell Johnson has noted, perhaps it would be more apt for the confession to be: *Christ has died, Christ is risen, Christ is reigning, Christ will come again*. This acclamation captures the present work of Christ. But either way, we affirm the ascension and the current reign of Christ is our confession and for us, the gospel—the good news that we proclaim week in and week out.

5. Calvin, *Institutes*, Book II, Ch. XVI, #14.

The Six Redemptive Acts of God in Christ Jesus

Pentecost and the Ascension

When we consider the salvation of God in Christ, we need to unequivocally affirm that Pentecost is as essential as each of the other redemptive acts. Without Pentecost it would all be for naught. All that transpired till then would be but at most an interesting sidenote in human history. The full benefits or effects of what God did in Christ in assuming human flesh, in going to the cross, and in the triumph of the resurrection and the ascension, is fulfilled in the church and in the cosmos by the Spirit. The Holy Spirit is the Spirit who makes the ascended Christ present.

And so, we celebrate Pentecost Sunday and with open and eager hearts pray "come Holy Spirit come, be present to us: fill us, anoint us, empower us, heal us and make all things new." We pray this prayer with a crucial assumption: that the Spirit is the Spirit of Christ and very specifically that the Spirit is the sent by the Father to bring glory to the ascended Lord (John 16:14). Thus when we pray to the Father through our high priest, we pray in the Spirit. And further, when in Christ all things are being reconciled to the Creator it is all through the grace of the Spirit. And in our participation in the mission purposes of God in the church and in the world, we are in turn called, gifted, guided, and empowered by the Spirit.

Thus, of course, the only Spirit we know is the Spirit who is given following the ascension, the very Spirit by which and through which we are in fellowship with the ascended Christ. We could easily make the case that the full meaning of Pentecost is nothing other than that we celebrate the gift of the Spirit by which and through whom we know the full meaning and significance of the ascension. The Spirit makes the living and ascended Lord present to the church and to the world.

It is noteworthy that on the Day of Pentecost the sermon preached by Peter makes reference to the gift of the Spirit—of course—but the central point that Peter makes is that the crucified and risen Lord is now ascended and is seated at the right hand of God (Acts 2:22–36). In the Spirit we worship the ascended Christ; in the Spirit we serve Christ and participate in the kingdom purposes of Christ in the world.

And so we always hold to this sequence between the ascension and Pentecost. The two events in salvation history must each be understood in light of the other: they are twinned. The ascension precedes and anticipates Pentecost and gives meaning to Pentecost. And Pentecost is the necessary counterpart to the ascension—necessary such that Jesus told his disciples to "wait." Yes, all authority has been given to Christ Jesus and, yes, the disciples are to be witnesses to the reign of God in Christ. However, it is all by and through the Spirit that this happens.

And yet, when we pray "come holy Spirit, come" it is that the longing of the church would be fulfilled: that we would see Jesus more fully, that we would know more deeply the love of God in Christ and that the purposes—the will of God in Christ—would be fulfilled in our lives and in the world. It is to this end that we seek the grace of the Spirit.

The following cannot be stated forcefully enough: Christian spirituality is then not pneumo-centered but Christ-centered. Or, to use more specific or technical language, our understanding and experience of the Spirit is deeply *christological*. We know we have received the grace of Spirit not because of ecstatic experience or heightened emotion but because Christ is glorified in us and through us. It all comes back to the ascension. The evidence that we are filled with the Spirit is not heightened emotional experience but that in our worship we know Jesus more fully, love him more ardently, and hear his voice, the voice by which we are called into life and mission.

The fullness of the Spirit in our lives—in our worship and witness—is evident in the quality and character of our fellowship with the ascended Christ Jesus. And the goal of the spiritual life and journey is simply this: union with Christ—made possible and effected in us by the Spirit. But it is still ultimately union with Christ. Our longing and aspiration is "Christ in you the hope of glory" (Col 1:27). Our shared worship might open with the prayer, "come Holy Spirit, come"—an apt and fitting prayer when we gather for the liturgy of the Christian community. But it is all to this end: that we would see Jesus—very specifically, that we would see Jesus, high and lifted up, seated on the throne.

This needs to be made so very clear. The danger is that if even if Jesus is named and celebrated, in a pneumo-centered worship and piety the Jesus in question is either no more than a projection of our own longings and desires or it is a spiritualized "Jesus," not the incarnate crucified and suffering Lord—the immolated lamb.

The Second Coming and the Ascension

The final redemptive act is the revelation of the ascended Christ—the consummation, the apocalypse—the aptly named "second coming". This is the promise fulfilled—spoken of by the angels at the ascension. Jesus had just

The Six Redemptive Acts of God in Christ Jesus

departed, and they assured the disciples that he would return and every knee would bow and every tongue confess that Jesus is Lord (Phil 2:10).

This is a redemptive act in its own right, of course; it is the fulfillment of all that God has been doing in Christ Jesus. And yet, the nuance or phrasing here is also so very important. It is not that Jesus becomes king on this day. Rather, it is *revealed* that he is king: the Father has already exalted him and given him the name that is above every name (Phil 2:9). Thus, the consummation of the kingdom, which is yet to come, is in many respects the revelation of what *already* is the case: Christ is now the ascended Lord.

He is ascended as the incarnate, crucified, and risen Lord who then, in turn, is the means by which the Spirit is known and received and, further, as the one who will in due time return to consummate his reign. On that day all creation will see and know and experience what Christian believers already know and confess: Christ Jesus is Lord. The Christian community gathers week in and week out to declare this reality and ascribe to Christ our unbounded praise and adoration even though this has not been fully revealed—not yet at least. But what shapes the common or shared life of the church is the conviction that this will happen. And so we live and worship and work with this assumption: that what we know now by faith we will then know by sight. We will, in the language of the apostle, see Christ face to face (1 Cor 13:12). And yet, without discounting this moment, it is but the revelation of what is already the case: that Christ is the ascended Lord and even now is the one who merits all glory, honor, and praise. Even now.

The best way to pray "even so, come Lord Jesus," the very best way to anticipate the triumph of God in Christ at the second coming, is to live now, *today* and every day, with our minds set above—to live by faith with a resilient hopefulness, sustained by a real-time encounter with Christ in the meantime, to live now in dynamic union, in worship and work, with the ascended Christ.

To summarize: the ascension gives ultimate meaning to each of the other acts of God in Christ. And yet, more needs to be said—something vitally important. While we might affirm that all the great acts of God in Christ coalesce in the ascension, they are not conflated in the ascension. They each have integrity in their own right and they each merit our attention. They are not lost or subsumed by the ascension. The incarnation, the cross, the resurrection, Pentecost—each of them merits our time and attention. We rightly celebrate six great acts of redemption; each is significant in its own right even if we make the case that each needs to be viewed and appreciated in light of the ascension. The incarnation, for example, is celebrated and affirmed and preached, even if we do so in anticipation of the ascension. In so doing we affirm the deeply human and physical—the fleshly—person that is Christ Jesus. And we resist all theologies or spiritualities that undercut or dismiss a genuinely Christian perspective on life and work—spiritualities that arise when the embodiment of Christ himself is downplayed.

And further, we do celebrate Pentecost and the outpouring of the gift of the Spirit. Pentecost is not a mere blip on the radar screen, it is a tremendous triumph of grace. As such, Pentecost Sunday is a grand event in the annual life cycle of the church. We very intentionally celebrate this day and speak of the gift of the Spirit because Christian community needs to have a pneumatology sufficient for navigating the complexities of living in the light of the ascension. To make any sense of life and ministry in this phase of redemptive history, when the kingdom has come but is yet to come, is with a vibrant and fulsome pneumatology. And thus we pray, "Come Holy Spirit, Come."

Living in the Reality of the Ascension

If the whole of Christ's redemptive work coalesces in the ascension, why would it not follow that the high point in the church calendar is not so much Advent and Christmas or Holy Week with the Triduum of Maundy Thursday, Good Friday, and Easter, but rather the dual feast celebration of ascension and Pentecost—the ten-day window in the annual church calendar when it all comes together? Rather than it feeling like a low point in calendar, if it is even acknowledged, competing for air time with Mother's Day? Might this instead become the ultimate celebration of the church—the high point in the church calendar?

Why, perchance, does Palm Sunday get more attention and energy than Ascension Sunday with a typical Christian congregation? Palm Sunday was actually a tragic day when all the celebration was for naught and those who waved the palms ultimately were soon crowded out by those who denounced Jesus and insisted "crucify him, crucify him!" I would not want to take away from the delight and joy of Palm Sunday—but merely observe the irony: perhaps Ascension Sunday would be the more fitting day to dance and celebrate and have a joyful procession. Why not take all

The Six Redemptive Acts of God in Christ Jesus

that we typically do on Palm Sunday and save it for *this* day—forty days after Easter?

We would do so to this end: that this—the ascension—is now the focus and dynamic of the Christian church. The ascension gives definition and purpose to our worship, to our individual prayers, to the mission of God in the world, and to the vocation of the individual Christian. And it is the ultimate reference when it comes to our identity as the people of God.

The ascension becomes the lens through which our lives and our world are viewed: we see everything in life, relationships, and work through this perspective, this worldview. It is like a set of glasses through which we make sense and meaning of all of life. It is the lens through which we enter into worship: our common prayers, our liturgies, our shared worship, each is a real-time encounter with the risen and ascended Lord Jesus Christ. And our personal prayer, our solitary prayers, are moments of genuine encounter—what some speak of as contemplation—a heartfelt knowing and seeing of Christ Jesus.

And then, consider that the mission of the church is to witness to this reality—yes, to the incarnation and the cross and, yes, to the reality of the resurrection, but ultimately and finally to this: the good news of the reign of God in Christ. And our sense of both our personal prayers and our vocation is that in our lives and in our daily experience, we can and do live in response to the calling and empowerment of the ascended Lord. Our work in the world is in response to his call.

What follows is an articulation of what this might mean—that is, what it might mean that what shapes forms and informs our lives is the reality of the ascension: what it means to "set our hearts and minds on things above" (Col 3:1–2); what it means to seek first the kingdom of God (Matt 6:33); what it means to speak in the present and consider that the ascension is a current existential reality in the life of the church. We ask: What does it mean to us—today, now, in real time—to live in the light of the ascension? What does it mean to have a vision of the ascended Lord that forms and informs our lives, our work and our witness, including the shared life we have in community as the church?

Rather than looking back to the cross, we look to the crucified one who now, in real time, is present to us in our worship and our prayer. Rather than looking ahead to when he will appear at the consummation of the kingdom we anticipate that grand event but live now, daily, with our eyes fixed on Jesus—yes, the eyes of faith, yes, the eyes of our hearts, but *this* is our current reality. This is what it means to live now, in this time and in this place, in dynamic relationship with Christ Jesus, fulfilling the call of Hebrews 3:1: "Therefore, holy brothers and sisters, who share in the heavenly calling, fix your thoughts on Jesus, whom we acknowledge as our apostle and high priest."

All of this is only possible if and as we learn what it means to live with a dual identity. We are citizens of the earth and citizens of heaven. On the one hand, our primary orientation is towards the reign of Christ—the kingdom of God. Jesus encourages his disciples to seek first the kingdom of God. There is, in other words, a fundamental vision for life and worship and work that shapes, forms, and informs our daily lives. We are a people whose identity, focus, and priority is the reign of the ascended Christ. We seek the kingdom; we live in light of the kingdom; we witness to the kingdom. This in no way takes away from the vitality and importance of the church in the redemptive purposes of God. The church is the gathering of the people who collectively witness to the kingdom. The church is a alternative community—with values and a vision that is shaped by this transcendent vision.

The church is the gathering of the people who have chosen to live in light of the ascension and as such, collectively embody what it means—what it might look like—that the kingdom has come. And the prayer of the Christian and the prayer of the church is simply this: "thy kingdom come, thy will be done on earth as it is in heaven." This does not put is in an adversarial posture towards our culture and the societies of which we are a part; rather it actually frees us to "seek the peace" of the cities and places in which God has providentially placed us (Jer 29:1–7).

This is why reading and preaching and teaching the parables of Jesus is so important and vital in the life of the church. They often open with some variation of "the kingdom of God is like . . ." and the teaching is precisely along these lines: that the kingdom of God has come and that now we live with this dual identity of those who live now in the "already" of the kingdom but equally as those who know that the kingdom will come in fullness in due time. The parables give us insight into what it means to live "in the meantime."

What makes the church the church is the ascension.[6] The church is not merely a gathering of individuals who have found forgiveness in the cross

---

6. Thus, the reference earlier to Douglas Farrow and his seminal publication *Ascension and Ecclesia*. This follows: if we speak of the ascension we necessarily speak of what it means to be the church.

The Six Redemptive Acts of God in Christ Jesus

and happen to be in the same place at the same time. Rather, the church is the body of Christ—the living and embodied witness to the reign of Christ here on earth; and what makes the church the church is that Christ is ascended. In and through the ascension, Christ Jesus becomes Lord and head of the church; with the ascension, the church—as a collective—is in organic and dynamic fellowship with Christ Jesus. Thus the Acts of the Apostles opens with the ascension. And Stephen encounters the ascended Christ at his martyrdom; Paul in like manner, meets Christ, in real time, on the road to Damascus. The ascension is precisely the Christ event that gives meaning to the identity and mission of the church as it is played out in both the common life and the mission of the church in the book of Acts.

Thus, when the ascension is our point of existential engagement with the work of Christ—a real-time engagement with Christ and the redemptive work of Christ—the implications are enormous. Our lives are without doubt marked by the historical reality of the life, death, and resurrection of Christ Jesus. Past tense. Further, we live in anticipation of the day when Christ Jesus will be revealed—at the consummation of the kingdom. Future tense. The past marks us; the future beckons us and is the basis for our living hope. But then, confident of what has happened in the past and confident of what will happen in the future, we are fully present to the here and now: we live intentionally in light of the ascended Christ and in the fullness of the Spirit.

The ascension defines our worship and our work. Our worship is an encounter with the incarnate, crucified, and ascended Lord—a worship that is mediated by and empowered by the Spirit, a worship that anticipates the consummation of the kingdom at the end of history. But crucial here is to appreciate that we are in the world as those who have been in worship; but also, we come to worship as those who have been and are in the world. Our worship, then, is not escapist—either in looking back or forward or even in looking "up." Yes, we look back to the cross and resurrection; and, yes, we look ahead to the consummation. But most of all, we are *here*—ready and willing and empowered to see our world more clearly and engage our world with greater conviction and courage as we in word and deed witness to the reign of the ascended Christ.

And so worship leads to mission: mission as an act of response to the call of Christ and as participation with Christ in announcing the reign of God in the cosmos. Mission flows from the worship, which is why we must insist on the priority of worship. Our engagement in the world is informed, fueled, and empowered by our encounter with Christ in the world. We are only truly in the world, in work and witness, if we are first and foremost worshippers and pray-ers.

The first disciples met Jesus on the Mount of Olives and, we read, worshipped him: and then from worship they heard the words "go into all the world and make disciples . . ." And it is no surprise that the early church was in worship (Acts 13:1–4) when they received the call to set aside Paul and Barnabas for missionary witness to Asia Minor. We go into the world as worshippers—specifically the worship of immediate encounter with the ascended Christ. But the converse is also true: we come to worship as those who have been in the world with Christ. Again, worship is not an escape from the world. A prayer retreat is not act of denial or rejection of the world and work to which we are called; it is rather a means by which, in the presence of Christ, we make some sense of what we have seen and experienced in our work and witness in the world.

So, what then does it mean to fully embrace the reality and implications of the ascension? At the very least, it means:

Our shared worship, as the people of God, will be a real-time encounter with Christ—in song, word, and table (for more on this theme, see chapter 3).

Our personal and solitary prayers will be a genuine meeting with Christ and we will grow in our capacity to know the voice of Jesus with the assurance of his love and the call of God on our lives (see chapter 4).

We will view the mission of the church as a witness to the reign of God in Christ—viewing the ascension as the announcement of the kingdom but with the full realization that the full expression is yet to come—and we will do mission "in the meantime" (see chapter 5).

We will view our personal vocation and work as a response to the call of God on our lives and as a participation in the work of Christ in the world (see chapter 6).

We will pray and sing the Psalms as the prayers and songs of those who live in the meaning of and who live and work and pray in alignment with the ascended Christ (see chapter 7).

And we will celebrate Ascension Day and Ascension Sunday as a high watermark in the Christian calendar.

3

The Character of Christian Worship

WORSHIP IS A REAL-TIME encounter with Christ Jesus, the ascended high priest and Lord. And it is our first response to the ascension. Every other dimension or aspect of the Christian experience flows from and is informed by worship. When the disciples met with Jesus immediately prior to the ascension, on the Mount of Olives, their first instinct was to worship him and in worshipping him they heard the call to make disciples of the nations. Their engagement with the world was the outcome of their encounter with Christ in worship. We must begin here. The church is first and foremost a *worshipping* community. Nothing so defines the identity of the church as this: a community of faith that gathers to meet, in real time, with the ascended Lord. What makes Christian community a *Christian* community, is that this people at this time have met Jesus. Together, they have been in his presence.

What makes this doubly significant is that our secular social or cultural context is marked by a loss of transcendence—the discounting of anything other than the immediate and material. Few have spoken to this as insightfully as philosopher Charles Taylor. At times he speaks of how "Western modernity is very inhospitable to the transcendent."[1] But he often goes further and speaks of the *denial* of transcendence.[2] And he notes how "exclusive humanism closes the transcendent window . . ." even though it

---

1. Taylor, *Catholic Modernity*, 25.
2. Taylor, *Catholic Modernity*, 25.

is the "crying need of the human heart . . ." At the same time, he notes, "human beings have an ineradicable bent to respond to something beyond life."[3] This suggests that the obstacles to belief in this social and cultural context are moral and spiritual rather than epistemic.

Worship cultivates and nurtures our capacity for transcendence. Thus perhaps it could be said that the most significant act of the church is precisely its insistence on and its regular participation in those actions and activities by which an awareness of transcendence is cultivated.

But we must stress, it is not just any transcendence. This is what it means to lead the church in worship. We bring the company of God's people into the transforming presence of the crucified, risen, and ascended Lord. We cultivate the capacity for and the actual experience of what Rudolf Otto speaks of as the *numinous*—as an awareness of the holy.[4] But to stress: it is not merely an experience of the nebulous other, something immaterial or mysterious. It is very specifically an encounter with a person, the risen and ascended Lord. And we need to affirm again and again that worship is fundamentally an *immediate* encounter with Christ; we do not merely speak *about* Christ, rather, Christ *meets* us—in a real-time encounter, as real and personal as his encounter with the two disciples on the road to Emmaus.

If Western secular modernity dismisses the transcendent, it is doubly imperative that the church demonstrate that this denial is a lie—that we can and will continue to witness to the reality of the "other." And we will continue to have an experience of the ascended Christ that, in turn, leads us in our witness to the world to a variation of what Philip said to Nathaniel (John 1:42ff): "Come and see." And what had Philip seen? He had met the Lord.

Thus, worship is not about an encounter with the Bible; nor is it merely a gathering of friends and the cultivation of community; nor it is about creating an event where evangelism can happen. In one sense it is all three of these: we do gather as the family of God, but if the gathering is not first and foremost an encounter with the ascended Lord, we are nothing but a religious club getting together with our friends and associates. And yes, the Christian community is the "fellowship of the word" and as such the Scriptures play an indispensable role in our common worship. But ultimately we gather not to meet the Bible but to meet Christ who is *revealed* to us through the ancient text. And, yes, worship is often a time and place where people are coming to faith in Christ; but this is so *because* they are meeting

---

3. Taylor, *Catholic Modernity*, 26–27.
4. Otto, *Idea of the Holy*, 8ff.

The Character of Christian Worship

Christ himself and not merely hearing about him; they are together as a community that is present to the ascended Lord.

As Philip said—and this is our message to the world: "Come and see; we have met the Lord." This is evangelism—witnessing to the reality of the transcendent. And nothing does this more powerfully than worship.

How do we foster an awareness of transcendence—more specifically, the consciousness awareness of the transcendent One? How to we bridge the two spheres of reality? How do we enter into the presence of the Triune God—together as a community of faith? What is the character of our shared worship—that is, the common prayers of the people of God?

I begin responding on the premise that the prayers of the individual Christian are the complement to and derivative of the prayers of the church. When we are alone in our prayers, we are alone as those who are also in community. We pray as individuals and encounter the risen and ascended Lord on our own—personally and intimately. But we do so as those who also meet Christ in real time and in the company of others—God's people. Our personal solitary prayer is the essential complement to our worship and prayer with others.

And we ask: can we know, as a community, the grace of a real-time encounter with the ascended Christ? Our response has to be a tentative "yes" at most; we cannot presume that we have a corner on heaven. And further we know that it is possible to secularize Christian worship—especially in our highly consumerist context—such that the presence of Christ is either lost or diminished. And yet, the witness of the Scriptures and the experience of the church over two thousand years affirms unequivocally that this can happen. We can meet God in Christ. But we need to be intentional and appreciate that there is a pathway or liturgy by which we approach the throne of grace. We do not presume to know how to encounter God. And thus we lean into the historic witness of the church. And in so doing we provide guidance to those who lead worship and to each of us as worshippers.

Three Elements of Christian Worship[5]

We can, of course, speak of diverse ways in which different Christian traditions foster transcendence. But on the whole, the weight and breadth of the

---

5. The Psalms are integral to our worship—as well as our personal prayers; and as such I have chosen to devote a whole chapter to the role of the Psalms (chapter 7) in the worship of those who seek to know, love, and serve Christ—to meet the ascended

historical witness, with few exceptions, are that there are three essential building blocks or elements to Christian worship—three vehicles, means of grace, by which we are brought into the presence of Christ. These are worship in song, worship as the engagement with the Scriptures, and worship at the gathering at the table.

First, worship in song—taking at face value the call of the Psalms and of the Epistle to the Colossians:

> Make a joyful noise to the Lord, all the earth.
> Serve the Lord with gladness; come into his presence with singing.
> Enter his gates with thanksgiving; and his courts with praise.
> (Psalm 100: 1, 2, 4).
>
> .... with gratitude in your hearts sing psalms, hymns, and spiritual songs to God. (Col 3:16)

Second, we can reference the remarkable meeting with Jesus on the road to Emmaus, where after their encounter they reported to the others:

> "Were not our hearts burning within us while he was talking to us on the road, while he was opening the scriptures to us?" ... Then they told what had happened on the road and how he had been made known to them in the breaking of the bread. (Luke 24:32, 35)

They noted: "were not our hearts burning within us" as Jesus spoke to them on the road and opened the Scriptures to them. On the road the focus was the Word: they knew Jesus as their teacher, making sense of the history of God's redemptive work. And then they also celebrated how he had been made known to them in Emmaus—revealed to them—in the "breaking of the bread" (Luke 24: 32 and 35). And thus it is no surprise that, as we read in the book of Acts, the early church "devoted themselves to the apostles' teaching and fellowship, to the breaking of bread and the prayers" (Acts 2:42).

What this suggests is that these two fundamental acts anchor our worship and are a means, as with song, by which God's people encounter the ascended Christ. This is why ancient worship and contemporary forms of worship that follow the historic pattern are demarcated by word and table. Worship in song might come before or after or be interspersed between word and table. We enter into the presence of Christ in song; we attend to the word of the ascended Christ through the reading and proclamation of Scripture; and then Christ receives us and feeds us at the table. And the

---

Lord in real time. Then, assuming the Psalms as an integral part of our worship, we can speak to the essential elements of worship by which we are drawn into the presence of the ascended Christ.

critical dynamic of the gathering—of the event—and what makes worship transformative—is that the three function in tandem. We will consider each in their own right, beginning with music, but stressing that even music, however wonderful it is, assumes the overall shape of Christian worship that includes word and table. Each is a distinct contribution to the act of Christian worship and yet it is three together by which the faith community is drawn into the presence of the ascended Lord.

Worship in Song: The Arts, Notably Music, and Christian Worship

When we speak of cultivating an awareness of transcendence, and the capacity to be fully present to another sphere of reality, we must speak of artists in our midst. Through their work they play a crucial and indispensable role in our communities, cultivating our capacity to know and experience the ineffable.

British philosopher Roger Scruton, writing on the philosophy of aesthetics—of art and beauty—observes that through metaphor, allusion, and symbol art works to foster what he speaks of as "the sense of a higher order, in which the superficial contingencies and contradictions of existence are resolved." The arts point to the ineffable and makes it present to us.[6]

All the arts have the potential to foster this awareness of the other—whether it is architecture, the visual arts, dance, or theatre; whether it is the remarkable use of light in the art works of Caravaggio, or the turn of phrase in William Shakespeare's plays and sonnets, or Russian novelists and their extraordinary capacity to portray in fiction the character of the human predicament. But when we think of the three essential elements of Christian worship, we must speak about the importance and place of music—and ask: Can music do this? Can music bridge us into the company of the transcendent and ascended Christ? Can we, in the words of the psalmist (Psalm 100), literally enter into the presence of God through singing?

In response, Robert Webber observes that

> Music is an auditory stimulant that is capable of evoking an experience with the transcendent. In music we take ordinary sound and through its arrangement we are able to lift the hearer into the ineffable.[7]

---

6. Scruton, *Music as an Art*, 167.
7. Webber, *Ancient-Future Worship*, 109.

In the Meantime

Webber in particular speaks favorably of the music of Taizé, which, he observes, "breaks through the ordinary to the unknown."[8]

Scruton contends that there are many ways in which music is able to do this. First, the order of music "transforms sequences of sounds into melodies"[9] that draw us into a new gravitational field. As Scruton notes, music can be trivial and meaningless, but "real music" is a continuous action of both freedom and necessity; it has an inherent logic that opens to us up to a different "space." It creates its own emotional and intellectual zone and invites us into that zone. Time stands still. And thus, Scruton observes, "music is leading us out of this world into a transcendental reality that we would otherwise not encounter."[10] We are able to imagine contact with the transcendent.[11]

Music puts us in touch with another world,[12] and in this space we find solace, vindication, and healing.[13] Music becomes the vehicle by which we lift up our hearts, the very means by which we can transcend rationality. It is not that the arts and music in particular are irrational. Not for a moment. It is rather that this music is not *purely* a matter of intellect and logic, though I would quickly add that it should and can and must have intellectual integrity—or for the Christian, a theologically informed understanding of God and the world.

For Scruton, the ultimate expressions of this is the Western classic musical tradition, and the three giants are Bach, Mozart, and Beethoven.[14] Scruton gives particular attention to the string quartet. While fully appreciating that there are diverse musical forms and genres, he notes that the string quartet is a unique medium with four voices—two violins, a viola, and a cello—wherein there is a unique tonal treatment that mimics the four voices of a choir. And for him this is the greatest of musical forms in part because stringed instruments, in his estimation, have a unique authority "when it comes to exploring abstract forms"—with the powerful counterpoint between intimacy and new tonal regions.

---

8. Webber, *Ancient-Future Worship*, 109.
9. Scruton, *Music as an Art*, 82.
10. Scruton, *Music as an Art*, 82.
11. Scruton, *Music as an Art*, 83.
12. Scruton, *Music as an Art*, 83.
13. Scruton, *Music as an Art*, 83.
14. Scruton, *Music as an Art*, 128 (Scruton seeks to make the case that Schubert should also be in their company).

The Character of Christian Worship

For many this is what it means to be in worship: to lean into the Western classical tradition, whether is the organ music of Bach or those hymns of the faith that depend on everything from four-part harmony to echoes of Western classical musical heritage.

But what of the contemporary movement of a more popular genre of music for worship? Swee Hong Lin and Lester Ruth contend that part of the genius of contemporary worship music is this kind of intentionality: to bring worshippers into the presence of God through a specific sequence of songs, what they speak of as "flow." Lin and Ruth note that in the 1980s various Pentecostal and charismatic communities developed theological models of worship that viewed the sequence or flow of worship as a journey into the holy of holies—a sequence that included:

- Gathering songs that anticipate worship and serve to align heart and mind towards heaven and the encounter with Christ;
- Songs of approach, where we name the movements of our hearts—including our lament—but then enter into the presence of God with thanksgiving (as noted in Psalm 100 and elsewhere in the Psalter);
- Songs where we are fully present to God; we have arrived and are now capable for what follows, namely the capacity for silence before the divine presence; and,
- Intimate songs in which one was aware of being in a holy space.[15]

The above pattern or sequence assumes a tight management of time; it is seamless, with, as Lin and Ruth put it, no "dead space."[16] And in response we might ask: can a sequence of contemporary songs, accompanied by high tech presentation of the lyrics and an intentional use of diverse forms of lighting, bring a person and a people into the presence of a holy God? For many, this is the only hope for the church; they have long since abandoned historic liturgical models—Gothic architecture, the organ and hymnody, and the sequence hymns and songs interspersed with the two foundational elements of word and table. They find all of that to be too emotionally dry, formal, and thus neither relevant nor engaging for the majority of those who come for worship.

---

15. Lin and Ruth, *Lovin' on Jesus*, 33. I will use this simple sequence when I come to chapter 7 and reflect on the role of the Psalms in making us present to the ascended Christ.

16. Lin and Ruth, *Lovin' on Jesus*, 36.

But here is the rub. Music can and should cultivate transcendence and the interior encounter with the ineffable. But, as with all art forms, music can do the opposite; rather than drawing us into the presence of the ascended Lord, it can actually lower the bar. When music, as with all art, is mere sentimentality—not honest and nothing but hype, cliché, or kitsch—it feeds narcissism and diminishes the sense of the transcendent. Or, worse, it suggests the possibility or the thought or idea of the transcendent rather than actually bringing us into the presence of the ineffable. Or even worse, when the music—whether classical or contemporary, whether older hymns or newer worship songs—only fosters a self-referential affirmation of our feelings, the consequence is that we are self-absorbed rather than genuinely coming into an encounter with God. We leave worship with comfort but it is a false comfort.

In other words, music can pander. Joseph Pieper, quoting Kierkegaard, is sure that music can open a "path to the realm of silence."[17] And so, Pieper speaks of the formative power of music and how for Plato music was a "tool to form man's character."[18] But then, Pieper observes, music can so easily be nothing but amusement or entertainment. Music can so often be trivial, superficial, and nothing but banality, especially when it is nothing but, in his words, "happy sound" and a "numbing beat."[19] So, yes, music has the capacity to bring us into the holy place, but all too readily, music can also be nothing but noise or a false comfort. We feel good perhaps. We enjoy the beat or the guitar riff. But does it actually connect us with heaven?

Could it be that much religious music tries to *imitate* transcendence—by being loud and boisterous and even popular, with a heavy beat imitating rock—but all it does it grasp after rather than actually bring us to the presence of the ascended one? It barges in. It tries to force its way into the throne room rather than coming in with due caution and with an appreciation that once we are in, the only possible response is silence: that the arts at their best in the end foster not noise but silence—noting the call of the Habbakuk: "the Lord is in his holy temple; let all the earth be silent before him" (Hab 2:20). Liturgical leaders come to know that they do not need to fill every space and that silence is not dead space, but an opportunity to be fully present to the risen and ascended Lord. We cultivate the capacity

---

17. Pieper, *Only the Lover Sings*, 44.
18. Pieper, *Only the Lover Sings*, 47.
19. Pieper, *Only the Lover Sings*, 49–50.

for silence and stillness as a way by which we empower each individual Christian to grow in their capacity to hear the call of God on their lives.

The danger is that if we succumb to sentimentality and banality, we foster nothing but the illusion of transcendence much like a visit to Disneyland gives us the idea that we have transcended time and space and the mundanities of our lives. But the result is not a genuine encounter; and thus the experience is not a transforming one.

Or, as Scruton puts it, might we, in a consumerist culture with a propensity to see the world as the object of desire, fall into an easy entertainment that distracts rather than cultivates awe? Scruton contends that it is not the arguments of atheists that have undercut the sacred but the overall propensity to cheapen the attempted encounter with God with lower-grade attempts at art.[20]

How then do we respond? Perhaps the genius of future worship that truly brings the people of God into the presence of the ascended, transcendent Lord, will be worship that effectively integrates ancient and contemporary, old and new. I think of the call of Robert Webber in his *Ancient-Future Worship*: older and time-proven forms of worship in song *and* more recent contributions—both, in a sense, accountable to each other and the counterbalance to the other: both calling the other to excellence, with no kitsch, no banality, no sentimentality. And no nostalgia.[21]

Either way, the genius of worship will be that it captures something of the human predicament but with a profound confidence in the ultimate purposes of God in the cosmos. It is surely to capacity to sing "when sorrows like sea billows roll" while also affirming, in the very same hymn, that "it is well with my soul." We get beyond happy-clappy platitudes, false optimism, and mere pleasantries that do not reflect the human condition or predicament. We get beyond the false comfort of a familiar chord sequence. We get beyond the assumption that heightened emotional experience is the essence of worship, that if it feels good we have presumably met God.

In an interesting observation, John of the Cross warns his readers about the dangers of familiar sacred spaces or places. He notes that sometimes all that happens in those spaces is a kind of nostalgic memory of meeting God in that space. Our experience is not immediate but secondary—more the memory of meeting God rather than the actual encounter. And thus the suggestion that we should not be overly inclined to one particular place

---

20. Scruton, *Face of God*, 177–78.
21. Webber, *Ancient-Future Worship*.

or space that we associate with meeting God.[22] Might the same be said of music? For music to be able to do what it can do, we need to be flexible and open to new genres. With music as with special memories we can evoke the memory of transcendence but that is all it is—the memory that through this music we were drawn into heaven at some point in the past. And that thus we perhaps need to be challenged to allow different genres of music to draw us into the holy place.

If we feel most comfortable and most engaged with charismatic or Pentecostal worship songs, we choose to be present for evensong in the Anglican choral tradition; and if Palestrina at St. Mary's Pro-Cathedral in Dublin is about as good as it gets for us, then we open our hearts to the possibilities of grace at jazz vespers. And if our preferred mode is the Bach organ recital, we choose to slip into the last pew of the Abyssinian Baptist Church in Harlem, New York, where the motifs of the African American experience call for a profound lament as well as the wonder of grace of God.[23] And, of course, we are present to other forms, other genres and approaches to music and worship, not as judge or critic, but as one eager to open heart and mind to the potential for transcendence. We stay open and attentive and follow the lead of musicians and other artists who know what it means for their art to bring us into the high places.

The Ministry of the Word: The "Kerygma" as Immediate Encounter with Christ

From worship in song, we move to the ministry of the word. The grace we seek is captured by the line referenced by those who met Jesus on the road to Emmaus: "were not our hearts burning within us while he was talking

---

22. John of the Cross, *Ascent*, III.39.#3.

23. I have a particular appreciation for the Anglican choral tradition. Few things have so drawn my heart into heaven as weekly choral evensong at the local Anglican cathedral. But I have been in worship at the Central Alliance church in Temuco, Chile, where a jazz saxophonist clearly knew how to move from the local jazz club to the worship space and obviously understood his role as nothing but bringing worshippers into the presence of Christ. And I have been in the high Andes when the indigenous musicians make magic with their pan flutes—not as entertainment, but as comfort to the soul and as witness to the presence and glory of the transcendent—though they have the huge advantage of the backdrop of the magnificent peaks of Chimborazo and Cotopaxi and the rest of the Andean mountain range.

The Character of Christian Worship

to us on the road, while he was opening the scriptures to us?" (Luke 24:32). And the question is simply this: can we experience the same grace?

The ministry of the word is an integral and essential element of Christian worship. It does not stand alone; worship is not merely the reading of Scripture followed by the weekly sermon. Worship in song and worship at the table are the essential counterparts to the word. And yet, the word is indispensable. As worshippers we come into the presence of the ascended Christ and we come with open and eager hearts—with minds alert to hear and understand, to know and live the Word of Christ. We long to know what it means, in the language of Colossians 3:15, that "the word of Christ would dwell richly within us."

It is common to speak of this as a *kerygmatic* moment: the *kerygma* is the word proclaimed—the moment or event wherein heaven and earth are linked as the Scriptures are opened, in the context of worship, and the ancient text made plain. The use of the Greek word *kerygma* is meant to highlight that this is not merely someone talking or teaching or giving a religious speech. With this language we seek to communicate that we have moved into another zone. It is human speaking in alignment with the ancient text.

The genius of the event in the life of the people of God is the continuity between the incarnate Word and the written word. Much is lost both in the meaning of the text and the transformational encounter with the text when the Scriptures are preached as mere letter and preached as an end in themselves rather than as a means by which Christ is revealed and known and thus heard. Much is lost and very little is gained when the Bible is but a tool, a weapon—what is often called "biblical preaching"—to set people right, to fix things. This is mere morality, mere biblical principles, mere truth that needs to be obeyed. Some of the worst examples of this are justified by the language of the word of God as a "sword."

Rather, the wonder of preaching is that Christ is made present: what the preacher longs for is that each person present would hear and know Jesus a little more fully, love Jesus a little more deeply, and feel equipped to serve Jesus more generously. The encounter is not ultimately with the Bible but with the one who is revealed through the Scriptures.

Preachers typically long to wow the crowd, be amazing and awesome, speak with a growing crescendo of intensity and volume, to shake the rafters and bring down fire and conclude with an audience having "felt" the immediacy of heaven. This is a misguided aspiration that we can lay aside. When the encounter with the transcendence happens, and it does happen, it comes merely because the preacher stayed with the text, explicated it as best as she could with an apt illustration here or there, and with compassion and intelligence and creativity. She has made the ancient text present to the people of God at this time and in this place.

What makes for good and effective preaching that draws us into the presence of the ascended Christ is not hype or even "charisma" per se. The grace of the moment when the Scriptures are opened and read and when the person set aside for this ministry steps into the podium or the pulpit is hard to explain. But when it happens, it is an encounter with transcendence; and those present for the reading and proclamation can each in our own hearts hear the voice of Jesus (John 10).

And so we ask: What makes the Sunday sermon, the homily, the preaching of the word, an event of transcendence—a kerygmatic event? Specifically, what *does* it mean to preach—to speak, to proclaim truth—in a time when there is a widespread ambivalence about public speaking in general—an era or season where preaching is viewed to be nothing but words, words, and more words, words that have no power or significance or weight—a time where words are cheap and where pathological liars are elected to public office. How do we think about preaching in such a time and think of it as fostering our capacity for transcendence, for an encounter with the ascended Lord? In asking this question, we can speak to both the preacher and the hearer in that both need to be full participants in this vehicle of grace.

To the preacher we say: While preaching is certainly a rhetorical event, preaching that brings us into the presence of Christ does not mean hype or gratuitous entertainment. Perhaps we follow the example of Jesus himself, and resolve to do little if any more than this: to open the Scriptures for those who are present (see Luke 24:32). As preachers we are merely making the ancient text present and in so doing opening up the potential for the living Christ to be present to the people of God, trusting in the interplay of word and Spirit and not in our capacity for rhetoric. We do not need to use the word "should," or say such things as "let me encourage you . . ." We have no need to use gratuitous humor or touching stories that are ultimately incidental to the word for that day. We avoid clichés and religious jargon. We shun platitudes. We choose plain speech—timely, honest, clear, and accessible. We are not singlehandedly trying to link earth and heaven through the sheer force of personality; we are just making plain the witness of Scripture.

The Character of Christian Worship

Most of all, the genius of ministry of the word is a deep confidence in the capacity of the word to fulfill the purposes for which God has sent it. As preachers, we open the text, make it plain, perhaps on some level explain the text, but then in the end we trust the Spirit to do what only the Spirit can do. Simple, clear, concise, and most of all, dependent on the unique work of the Spirit in the hearts of the hearers—for them to know and respond to the voice of Jesus. We are not merely talking about Jesus—well, yes of course, we talk about Jesus—but the main agenda is for the people of God to *hear* Jesus through the Scriptures. Through the proclamation of the ancient text we see and know and feel that Christ reigns. The gospel of the kingdom is preached—good news for those who feel the fragmentation and uncertainty of life on planet Earth. As the apostle Paul *stressed*, it is not about eloquence, but rather that they did not preach themselves but Christ Jesus as Lord (2 Cor 4:5).

In his fascinating study of the history and character of choral evensong in the Anglican liturgical tradition, Simon Reynolds speaks to the homily that is part of such an event and notes that:

> Delivering a sermon at Evensong can be a delicate balancing act: partly because of the attractions of Choral Evensong (especially on weekdays) is precisely the fact that there is no sermon; and because a period of extended speech can often feel out of place in a service that is more of a contemplative—rather than instructive—character. Nonetheless, if approached with a degree of pastoral insight and theological imagination, using no more words that are actually necessary, a sermon at Evensong can be an effective way of inviting worshippers to cultivate a God-centred view of the world they inhabit, with all its stresses and opportunities.[24]

I wonder if what Reynolds says about evensong might actually apply to all preaching in all contexts, especially when he adds: "The best sermons will always be as carefully crafted as the prayer, poetry, architecture and music that characterizes the rest of Evensong."[25] And not to be missed is his observation: "no more words than necessary."

Here are some good rules of rules of thumb for the contemporary preacher.[26] Brevity is a virtue; longer is not better. Might eighteen minutes

---

24. Reynolds, *Lighten Our Darkness*, 70.
25. Reynolds, *Lighten Our Darkness*, 70
26. For much of this paragraph I lean into the insights of colleague Mark Buchanan, from his essay, "Preaching Now and Then."

be the outer limit to say what needs to be said? We say no more than needs to be said. We avoid being overly didactic. Preaching will always have a teaching element to it, but this is not a mini lecture. There is a place for the lecture, for the extended consideration of a biblical text—with focused exegesis and cultural analysis. But not in a sermon that is meant to draw hearers into the presence of God.[27] Finally, avoid the temptation to use the bully pulpit to score moralistic points.

Then, further, we bring advice not only to the preacher but to the hearer as well. Can we each, when we are in worship and attend to the oral reading of Scripture and to the preaching, come with open hands and what the psalmist speaks of as a clean heart? We come with a simple prayer that we say in the quietness and privacy of our own thoughts: "Come, Lord Jesus, that I might hear your voice and your word to me for today." Or, "What would you have me, your servant, hear through this?"

What makes preaching the kerygma is this very duality: the preacher tending to the ancient text and making it present; and the people of God attentive to how Christ is present to them through this word. We let go of anger and receive the word with meekness (Jas 1:21). We move beyond any need to be entertained knowing that this shared time has a different agenda: to know the voice of Jesus. With open hands and hearts lifted up, we are not defaulting into critic mode of this morning's sermon, but simply asking: "What is the word of Jesus to me today?"

The arts—in particular music (the hymns, songs, and spiritual songs)—frame this encounter with the word. We sing and in so doing lift up our hearts in anticipation of the reading and proclamation of the ancient text. And then we sing in response to the proclaimed word: all to this end, that the Word of Christ would dwell within us—Colossians 3:16, "Let the word of Christ dwell in you richly"—as women and men who have heard the voice of Jesus, the risen and ascended Lord.

---

27. Thus I would add to Buchanan these guidelines: just one point (keep it simple) and avoid the use of high-tech screen visuals, which often are nothing but a distraction. And, perhaps most of all, be autobiographical to illustrate the text but remember that in the end it is not about you and you are not the hero of the story. And then also be very attentive to the opening and the conclusion.

The Character of Christian Worship

The Table Where Christ Hosts Us at the Holy Meal

For the ancient church, the table was the essential counterpart to the ministry of the word: they devoted themselves to the apostles' teaching and as well to the "breaking of bread" as a weekly practice (Acts 2:42 and 20:7). The table for many Christians is the high point of encounter with Christ; it is here, at the table, that Christ is known and recognized, in the language of Luke 24. The table is not either occasional or optional. We meet Christ in song and the word, but nowhere is the encounter with the ascended Lord more evident than at the table. Christ hosts us; Christ meets us at the table of mercy; Christ feeds us.

On the meaning and significance of the ascension, this is where all of this gets personal for me. My appreciation of the importance of the ascension was definitely informed by the regular references to the ascension by Professor John Dahms, when I was a seminary student. And most of us who are eager to give this matter more attention recognize our indebtedness Douglas Farrow's *Ascension and Ecclesia*. And yet the pivotal moment for me came at the table. I grew up with in a church tradition that insisted that nothing and no more happens at the meal than our remembrance of what Christ had done for us. We were "partaking" with a fear of some level of judgment if we did not quite get it right.

But then I was visiting a church of a tradition different from that in which I had been raised. And there, at the front, with open hands, I knew I was being enveloped by the mercy of God and being fed by Christ's very self. This was food for the road, granted by a benevolent Lord who loved me to the core of my being. That changed everything. I had met Christ in real time. I knew that in this holy meal we look back to the cross. And I knew that we also look ahead to the consummation of the kingdom. But then and there I came to see that we lift up our hearts in the immediate and now, in this time and in this place, and the ascended Lord Christ meets us. It is an encounter as personal and real as that which the two had with Christ in Emmaus. We are not merely *thinking* about Jesus; we are not merely *remembering* what Christ has done for us; we are *meeting* the ascended Lord who hosts this holy meal.

For many Christian communities much of this is lost out of an attempt to be casual, informal, and accessible. It is a questionable if not actually misguided attempt to keep it interesting through novel approaches to the table. But the genius of the table is precisely that it is sacramental—unapologetically so. Through this act, we are transcending time and space;

we are entering into another sphere of life and reality. Minimizing this is counterintuitive. We need to sustain a sense of wonder—the sheer moment of the occasion: that the ascended Lord meets us at table and welcomes us with open arms. Nothing is gained and much is lost by discounting the potential for each worshipper, in the company of the faithful, to meet and know Christ who hosts us at this holy meal.

For many of us coming out of the low church or free church traditions—whether Wesleyan or Calvinist or Holiness or Pentecostal—it is high time we get over our inclination to fear anything that strikes as Orthodox or Catholic or high Anglican, and realize that these traditions are on to something that we all so urgently need. Without for a moment discounting the ministry of music and song and the importance of preaching (I am a preacher) for many of us, this is the moment: this is where and how we meet Christ and know the full force of what Jesus himself said at the ascension: "Lo, I am with you always." And as noted, it is food for the road—the nourishment we need to stay the course, to be in but not of the world, to be all that we are called to be "in the meantime."

Is it any wonder that so many of those from low church traditions are migrating down the road to Orthodox, Catholic, and Anglican church communities? They simply do not buy the practice of "once a month on the first Sunday of the month," which they have come to see has no biblical or theological basis. And they refuse to countenance that if they celebrate the table more often, they will "appear" to be Catholic because that is what Catholics do! This contention has no traction with them. They want the biblical model of "they devoted themselves to the breaking of the bread." And they know they need it if they are going to navigate life and work and witness "in the meantime."

For those who affirm the legitimacy of an open table—that all who are present are welcome to participate—the principle advocated by John Wesley and others comes into play: that the Lord's Supper is not merely a nurturing sacrament but also a *converting sacrament*—a means by which the ascended Lord welcomes seekers into his company and presence and the experience of his grace.

Song, word, and table. Can we also speak of *silence* as indispensable to Christian worship? We seek the grace where it can be said to us, "Be still and know" (Ps 46); be still and fully present; be still and in quietness attend and be at peace with the ineffable. Silence is not dead space, but rather the essential space where in a world of distraction we learn to be still and attend to the presence of Christ in our midst.

The Character of Christian Worship

The House of Worship

What "houses" our worship—in song, word, and table? Does location matter? Can we speak of sacred buildings or rooms? Can we speak of the importance of architecture and liturgical space? For centuries, both in Europe and beyond, churches were built with a focus on fostering a sense of the sacred—the ineffable. William McAlpine in his reflections on the importance of space notes that much of the Western church and evangelicalism in particular has concluded that space is, as he puts it, of "secondary importance."[28] In response, he writes: "the church cannot thrive, let alone fulfill its mission in the twenty-first century, without a comprehensive understanding of the praxis component inherent in a theology and hermeneutic of the built environment."[29]

In a similar vein, Robert Webber also contended that space matters and suggested in the 1980s that evangelicals could "neutralize space to make the seeker more comfortable."[30] But then he quickly notes that this will not work in a postmodern world where, instead, "the inquirer needs to be immersed within a space that bespeaks the Christian faith."[31] Space, he observes, is the medium by which we connect the known and the unknown.[32]

In speaking of the elements of Christian worship, we can recognize that architecture and design play a vital part in fostering transcendence. We need those who know how to design a space that fosters an awareness of the ascended Lord—sacred space, or what is sometimes spoken of as *thin* space: a spatial location where there is a unique awareness that one is in the presence of Christ. And I am personally so grateful for those church traditions where the building or facility for worship is open during the week and in the heart of the city there is a quiet space where I can slip in for a few moments of prayer and silence between the demands and meetings of that day.

Lift Up Your Hearts

All of this is about the orientation of the heart. We cannot stress this enough: that in coming to worship—in song, and to the word, and to the table—we

---

28. McAlpine, *Sacred Space for the Missional Church*, 11.
29. McAlpine, *Sacred Space for the Missional Church*, 11.
30. Webber, *Ancient-Future Faith*, 108.
31. Webber, *Ancient-Future Faith*, 108.
32. Webber, *Ancient-Future Faith*, 108.

hear the call "lift up your hearts" with the apt response, "we lift them to the Lord." Our worship in song is hearty, from the depths of our being. We come to the word, in the language of the book of James, not with anger in our hearts, but with meekness given by the Spirit. This is the essential interior disposition with which we engage and receive the word so that, in the language of Colossians 3:15, the Word dwells in us richly. Indeed, the Colossians text makes a one-to-one linkage between the two—letting the word dwell richly within us as we sing psalms, hymns, and spiritual songs with gratitude.

And then we come to the table with an eagerness to receive bread and the cup—not half-heartedly, but with an lively childlike disposition.

For some, this is all signaled with our hands. In song, we lift our hands. In the reading and proclamation of the word, we are not taking notes or in a critical posture, but our hands reflect the disposition of our hearts: open and willing to hear what God is saying to us. And then at the table, our hands are open to receive the bread and the cup as what they are: the gifts of God for the people of God. Most of all we must stress that the genius of worship is an encounter with the benevolent God who in Christ is fostering within us the capacity to know the love of God. And thus we sing:

> Jesus, Thou Joy of Loving Hearts.
> Thou Fount of life, thou fount of all,
> From the best bliss that earth imparts,
> We turn unfilled to thee again.[33]

This is so in song but also in the ministry of the word. In preaching we are not beaten down or beaten up, but rather invited to live in the kingdom of light and in the freedom and joy of the reign of Christ. And in the table we encounter not a seat of judgment but a table of mercy. In real time we meet the ascended Lord and in the presence of Christ come to see and feel that God knows us, loves us, and that God is for us and not against us.

And then, we move into the world as those who have met Christ, in song, word, and table. But before we consider what it means to speak of the ascension and the mission of the church, we need to consider the essential counterpart to our common or shared worship and prayer: the personal and solitary prayers of the individual Christian.

---

33. "Jesus, Thou Joy of Loving Hearts," attributed to Bernard of Clairvaux (translated by Ray Palmer).

4

Personal and Solitary Prayer

THE ENCOUNTER WITH THE ascended Christ is always both/and. We know and meet Christ *together*, in community when we gather for shared worship. And we know and meet Christ *alone*, in our personal and solitary prayers. Both are essential and they are essential *together*. Common prayer needs the essential counterpart of our solitary prayers. Individual and personal prayer is only offered by those who are regularly participants in our common worship.

The question to consider is whether and how an individual and solitary Christian can know and experience a real-time encounter and relationship with Christ, as the ascended Lord. In speaking about prayer we need to reaffirm a fundamental assumption: that prayer is a means of our own formation in Christ—essential to what it means to "make disciples." Prayer is itself a transformative experience in which we are made new and know the healing grace of God. Prayer is itself a transformative encounter with Christ, a means by which the purposes of God are fulfilled in us. And thus the words of the apostle, speaking autobiographically, but then with regard for all who encounter the ascended Christ:

> And all of us, with unveiled faces, seeing the glory of the Lord as though reflected in a mirror, are being transformed into the same image from one degree of glory to another, for this comes from the Lord, the Spirit. (2 Cor 3:18)

Can our personal prayers be a means of our formation—maturing as disciples? And more, can our personal prayers foster our capacity to discern what we are called to do and know the courage to do what we are called to do?

Note then two basic questions: Can we, in our personal prayers, meet Christ Jesus, the ascended Lord, in real time? And second, can we in this encounter discern the calling of God on our lives—not a generic call, but the particular and specific vocation to which Jesus is inviting us?

In what follows, I am making an assumption: no one can do this for you. Personal prayer is a capacity that is fundamental to what it means to be a Christian and while we can and will pray for one another, the focus here is *your* encounter with the ascended Lord: to know Jesus, in real time, and to hear the voice of Jesus for you, at this time and in this place. Is this a grace that is given to all Christians—at least potentially so? Is this even to be expected? Can we learn about personal and solitary prayer from the history of the church and those who have been the great voices and teachers on the character of prayer?

Leaning into the Christian Mystical Tradition

For my own understanding and journey, I am indebted in part to the witness of a spiritual writer from my own denominational and spiritual tradition, A. W. Tozer—pastor in Chicago for many years and then later pastor of Avenue Road Alliance Church in Toronto. His writings continually come back to this theme or topic: the pursuit of God and the intimate knowledge of God. Much of his writing has an unfortunate side to it—his propensity to dismiss critical and intellectual engagement and the cultivation of a Christian mind. Rather than affirming both/and—head and heart, intellect and affect—Tozer often pits the one against the other even though in practice he clearly chooses to be thoughtful and theologically informed. And yet, for many of us the main contribution from Tozer is that he insisted that we flourish as Christian believers if and as there is a radical *receptivity* to God. That is, that the key to the Christian life is what he speaks of as "spiritual receptivity"—notably a longing for, a pursuit of, and as such an encounter with the face of God.[1]

In the introduction to his *Christian Book of Mystical Verse*, Tozer observes that the mystics in the spiritual history and heritage of the church

---

1. Tozer, *Pursuit of God*, 67.

Personal and Solitary Prayer

provide contemporary Christians with an essential witness to the possibility of this personal encounter with Christ. He took a lot of grief for this—for his willingness to turn to the mystical theologians of the church as guides to the spiritual life, specifically to the life of prayer. But he insisted that their vision for contemplative prayer was deeply consistent with the witness of the Scriptures—especially, but not only, in what we read in the Psalms.

Tozer fully acknowledges that his evangelical and more religiously conservative constituency (what he would speak of as his "fundamentalist" counterparts) might balk at words like *mystic* and *mystical*, but he urges his readers to recognize that what the mystics speak to is no more or less than the experience of notable characters in Scripture—from Moses to Elijah to David to Isaiah, to Paul and John in the New Testament. I would add this: the failure to appreciate the potential for this encounter with Christ is but further evidence that we do not recognize the full significance of the ascension and thus the call to the prayer of encounter with Christ in real time.

Encouraged by Tozer, I came to see the great mystical theologians as essential guides to prayer: from Augustine to Bernard of Clairvaux to Julian of Norwich, Thomas à Kempis, Francis de Sales, and many others, most of whom were pre-Reformation voices or writers who were part of the Catholic rather than Protestant world. I hesitated on some; I struggled to reconcile myself to Meister Eckhart, for example, and I have friends who have urged me not to give up on *The Cloud of Unknowing*. But in the process I discovered the giants, the three great Catholic Reformers of the sixteenth century, indispensable guides to prayer: Ignatius of Loyola, Teresa of Avila, and John of the Cross.

And yes, I use the word *indispensable* intentionally. In a secular age, might it be an imperative that now, more than ever, we live and move with grace, courage, and generosity in our world as those who know Christ intimately and personally? Rowan Williams, in his comments on prayer and spirituality in a secular age, makes a bold declaration: "contemplation is . . . an ontological necessity."[2] That is, we will not survive let alone thrive in the current social and cultural climate unless and until we cultivate this interior capacity. A. W. Tozer was prescient—planting the seeds in an earlier generation that would then come to flower for Christians who live and work generations later in a very different social context, one in which it is

---

2. Williams, *Silent Action*, 30. That statement is part of the fuller articulation, "Contemplation is not a religious exercise but an ontological necessity in the intense *personalism* of Christian faith . . ." (emphasis in original).

vital and essential that, as Tozer would insist, we lean into the wisdom of the mystical theological and spiritual tradition. These three great teachers, especially, have so much to offer to Christians who live and work and worship in a secular age.

The weight of the tradition has focused on what is typically thought of as a *sequence* in the development of the life of prayer. It is assumed at first that we are beginners, just learning the practice of prayer and that we mature, over time. The historic witness—or tradition—has spoken of three stages or phases to maturing prayer: the purgative, the illuminative, and the unitive. I use the language of stage or phase hesitantly, in that the experience of prayer is not like grade #1, #2, or #3 in elementary school. Growth in prayer is more organic and, in a sense, one never leaves the first stage behind. But one does mature in prayer; one grows up so that one comes to union with Christ and into fellowship with the Triune God. The Trinity is something that is lived. We do not merely talk about the Trinity or confess a Triune God or do a theological assessment of what it means to all God Triune. Rather, in our prayers we are drawn by the Spirit into union with Christ and thus into fellowship with the Father.

The goal or objective of the Christian life is not merely "what would Jesus do?" but to know Christ, and love him more deeply and serve him more generously, in response to the *particular* call of Christ on our lives. And yet we must highlight that this unfolds in the life of prayer slowly and through much inner wrestling. When we first become Christians, we are children—infants—in that we want Jesus to make us happy and healthy and solve our problems. We ask God to bless our efforts and help us be successful.

But as we mature we come into union with Christ, through the Spirit, and recognize that nothing matters more in life than this: to know Christ. Or, in the words of the apostle: "I want to know Christ and the power of his resurrection and the sharing of his sufferings by becoming like him in his death" (Phil 3:10). Or, as the apostle puts it in Colossians: "Christ in you, the hope of glory" (Col 1:27).

And yet it is important to stress that we come to this over time—over a lifetime of prayer with a disposition or posture of openness to God. This way of seeing and feeling is not a mere choice we make, though our receptivity to the work of God is essential. Rather, it is formed within us—slowly and gradually—through the *practice* of prayer. More specifically, I would note, it is the *habituated* practice. Wise Christians recognize that this can be a challenging and confusing journey. And so we turn to those who have

Personal and Solitary Prayer

been there, spiritual masters who have provided the church with a guide to prayer—specifically to contemplative prayer, the prayer of encounter. One place we can go—not the only place, for sure, but an invaluable resource—is the trio of Ignatius of Loyola, Teresa of Avila, and John of the Cross. I will reference other voices, but these are the heavyweights who distill the history and wisdom of the mystical tradition from prior centuries and uniquely inform the conversation and the experience of Christians even today.

Ignatius of Loyola (1491–1556) is best known for *The Spiritual Exercises of St. Ignatius of Loyola*. Over the centuries this has become an indispensable resource to so many Christians of many theological and spiritual traditions. It provides those who pray with a guide or order so that we come into an encounter with Christ in the privacy of our place of prayer.

Eventually Ignatius would found the Society of Jesus (Jesuits), a missionary or apostolic order with a high commitment to scholarship and learning. Jesuits are known for commitment to schools and universities. And yet, it is study and learning and scholarship that is informed by the encounter with the ascended Christ.

At age twenty, Teresa of Avila (1515–1582) entered a Carmelite monastery. In short order she had significant illness that plagued her for the rest of her life. Early on, though, she was reading spiritual masters, including Augustine and his *Confessions*. She testifies to how in 1554 she came to a new grace of intimate awareness of Christ in her life—a season in which she learned more fully about the character of contemplative prayer. By 1562 she was instrumental in the reformation and renewal of the Carmelite order while all along writing about and making sense of her own experience of prayer.

We have her autobiography and her more extended *The Way of Perfection*. But when it comes to her most mature teaching on prayer, we turn to *Las Moradas*, typically translated as *The Interior Castle*, or, in some translations, *The Dwelling Places*. It is her guide to the interior life, reflecting her conviction that our encounter with Christ is an internal one—in the inner recesses of our hearts. Both Teresa and Ignatius encourage their readers to meditate on the life and humanity of Jesus, convinced that the oh so very human Jesus of the Gospels is the very one whom we encounter in our prayers when we are present to the ascended Christ.[3]

In John of the Cross (1542–1591), we have perhaps the premier guide to prayer in the history of the church. Also from Spain, born not far from Avila, he was an avid student and scholar, attending the Jesuit College from

---

3. Teresa of Avila, *Interior Castle*, ¶399.

1559–63, during which time he was immersed in both Greek language and culture along with the Christian theological and spiritual tradition. In 1563, at age twenty, he entered the Carmelite religious order. In 1567 he headed to Salamanca to study at the university that at that time was considered the primary venue for critical theological study in that region. Like Teresa, he was also committed to reform for the order and for the church, and consequently he spent much of his life under threat from the Inquisition and even had an extended imprisonment in solitary confinement. But along the way, he wrote and continued to write, most notably on the theme of contemplative prayer. His most significant contributions to the topic are *The Ascent of Mount Carmel* and *Living Flame of Love*.

Part of the invaluable contribution is that John, while immersed in the Scriptures—particularly the Gospels—sought to make sense of his own experience of prayer. He never disparages the life of the mind and the importance of the intellectual life; he was both a New Testament scholar and a contemplative. And what we most learn from him is the primacy of personal prayer and that in prayer we encounter the love of God manifested to us through the crucified, risen, and ascended Christ.

What impresses us with Ignatius, Teresa, and John of the Cross is a common pattern: they draw on the wisdom of the centuries before them while also making sense of their own prayers. They speak of their own experience of prayer and seek to interpret it while drawing on the wisdom of those who have gone before.

Contemplation, Solitude, and Knowing the Love of God in Christ

When we distill the wisdom of these three key voices, what do we learn?

First and fundamentally, the entire mystical tradition assumes if not actually *presumes* the priority of solitary prayer: solitude is indispensable to the contemplative life and, more specifically, the presence and power of God in our lives, specifically the transforming knowledge of the love of God for us, is known in the context of our solitary prayers.

As noted, there were those who were very critical of A. W. Tozer and his call to attend to and learn from the mystical theological and spiritual tradition. That same or very similar resistance is equally present now—voices that protest that mysticism and solitary and interior prayer are inconsistent with the call of the Scriptures and that the faith is fundamentally

Personal and Solitary Prayer

a communal experience and further, that it is essentially a rational experience. Thus for example, we have Donald Bloesch, who would not only resist but actually condemn the mystical tradition. He contends:

> It cannot be denied that there is a fundamental incongruity between mysticism and biblical Christianity. In stark contrast to the biblical ethos, mysticism is uncompromisingly introspective. Its focus lies on the exploration of the depths of the soul, not the preaching of Christ to the masses.... Jesus mingled with people, whereas mystics elevate solitude over fellowship. This inward proclivity comes not from the Bible but from Platonism and Neoplatonism.[4]

In response, I want to say emphatically: yes, Professor Bloesch, it *can* be denied. And to ask him: have you read Ignatius or Teresa or John of the Cross? Have you truly engaged them? Ignatius founded one of the most powerful and influential missionary agencies in the history of the church; he was hardly "uncompromisingly introspective." John of the Cross and Teresa were both very much in community and, as must be stressed, while all three insist on the cultivation of the interior life and of solitary prayer, they assume—or better *presume*—one's participation in the life of the church. This would or should be evident to anyone who is reading their published work. Further, while they insist on solitary prayer, for all three this prayer is necessarily complemented by service in the world—but more, it is also an essential *precondition* to engagement with the world.

But, while the Bloesch caricature is flawed, we need to begin here: the heart of the matter is solitude—the individual encounter with Christ. As a member of the community of faith and as one engaged in the world, but still, as persons who know what it is to be alone in our prayers and able to hear the voice of he ascended Jesus. This is the essential capacity for service in a post-Christian and secular context. What A. W. Tozer would proclaim today if he was still with us is precisely this point: that in a secular age, interiority is essential and that the church urgently needs to lean into the wisdom of the mystical theological and spiritual tradition. And what we learn is that solitude is an indispensable complement to shared worship. Of the three key sixteenth-century voices, it is likely John who makes this most explicit: that the true contemplative is not merely a solitary pray-er,

---

4. Bloesch, *Spirituality Old and New*, 68. I am especially grateful to Daniel Harris for drawing this quote from Bloesch to my attention. While Bloesch himself is no longer with us, this perspective is very much still part of a common hesitation among many Christians to learn from the mystics.

but also a full participant in the life of the church. We are not hermits; we are in community; our solitary prayer is only authentic and a genuine encounter with Christ when it is the personal and individual counterpart to the common worship of the people of God. And we learn that solitude is the essential precursor and complement to our engagement with the world. The contemplative tradition assumes that we learn this: what it means to be alone with God; that solitude is an indispensable feature or element of the Christian life.

Solitude does not fuel narcissism; rather, authentic solitude fosters the capacity to be present to another—God's very self who is revealed to us in the ascended Christ. Thus solitude is not an end, but a means to an end: to know Christ and to hear his voice and be empowered in that encounter for the work to which we are called in the world. Solitude always has this orientation towards Christ. In prayer we are in solitude, but we are not alone; we are with the Lord. Our focus and orientation is with and for and toward Jesus.

Ignatius reminds us that any genuine and transformative engagement in our world flows from this encounter with the ascended Christ: we are in the world as worshippers, as pray-ers, as those who have met Christ in real time. In his classic, *The Spiritual Exercises of St. Ignatius of Loyola*, we have not a spiritual treatise per se, but a guide to prayer: a structure or a kind of order or liturgy to our prayers, a way to think and pray and respond to the inner work of the Spirit in our minds and hearts. The *Exercises* assume solitude and solitary prayer. Ignatius observes that:

> the more the soul is in solitude and seclusion, the more fit it renders itself to approach and be united with its Creator and Lord; and the more closely it is united with Him, the more it disposes itself to receive graces and gifts from the infinite goodness of its God.[5]

The language of "soul" would be typical as a way to speak of the interior life. But the main point is that this solitude is not an emptying of consciousness, but rather a solitary prayer in which and through which one meets Christ and knows Christ. And thus the exercises guide the pray-er through a series of imaginative encounters with Christ, through focused meditation on the Gospel scenes of Jesus with his disciples and others. And the pray-er is invited to read and pray the Gospel scenes and imagine themselves in those scenes, recognizing that the Christ of the Gospels who met

---

5. Ignatius, *Spiritual Exercises* ¶20.

Personal and Solitary Prayer

his disciples on the Sea of Galilee or the Mount of Transfiguration is the same Christ to whom and with whom we pray. In our praying, for example, the *Exercises* invite us to picture ourselves in the boat, in the storm, with the original disciples. We like them feel the full force of the response of Christ to our distress in the face of the storms in our lives. And we, now and in real time, in our own circumstances, hear the words of admonishment, "Why are you afraid, O men of little faith?" These are the words of Jesus to us today as men and women who face the challenges of our times.[6]

This approach to prayer demonstrates that there is a profound continuity between the Jesus of the Gospels and the Jesus who is now the ascended Lord. In our worship and in our prayer, we encounter the same Jesus who is revealed to us in the Gospels.

And nothing so marks solitary prayer as the awareness of the love of God for us in Christ. In our prayers, we see and experience God in Christ as benevolent: we know the love of God in Christ that is poured into our hearts by the Holy Spirit (see Rom 5:5). As children we might have sung "Jesus loves me . . . [because] the Bible tells me so," but what we come to learn is that in light of a personal encounter with Christ, we know the love of God in Christ because Christ has told us so! The love of God for us is not a matter of rational deduction from a text of Scripture; rather, the encounter with God and with the love of God in Christ is something that is known through the gracious work of the Spirit.

And coming back to Teresa, we note her major assumption: that our encounter with the ascended Lord is an *interior* reality and experience. This is what lies behind her central image of dwelling places—the *moradas*, the interior castle or space where Christ is abiding. Yes, Teresa writes in a way that invites her readers to hear the words of the apostle, to "set your minds on things that are above," and to look to Christ "who is seated at the right hand of God" (Col 1:1–2), so that indeed our lives are hidden with Christ in God (Col 1:3). And in so doing, Christ dwells in our hearts by faith (Eph 3:17). Teresa helps us know something of the reference of the apostle, in Colossians 1:27: "Christ in you the hope of glory."

What Teresa seeks to capture is precisely that we are in Christ as Christ is in us; that we are in union with the risen and ascended Lord, at the right hand of the Father, even as we experience the interior grace of Christ who is intimately present to our interior lives. For John, as with Teresa, the goal of prayer is the knowledge of God and the love of God. This is the true home

---

6. Ignatius, *Spiritual Exercises* ¶279.

for the soul: to dwell in the love of God. They both echo the earlier spiritual writer, Julian of Norwich, who when she writes on the love of God notes:

> For truly our loving God wants our souls to cling to him with all their might, and wants us to cling to his goodness forever. For of everything the heart could devise, this is what most pleases God and most readily benefits us; for our soul is so specially loved by him that is highest that it surpasses the knowledge of all beings— that is to say there is no being made that can know how much and how sweetly and how tenderly our Maker loves us.[7]

But, and here is where the contribution of John of the Cross is so noteworthy, the love of God "is not gentle, but afflictive."[8] It is a purgation; it is redemptive. It is not mere happy feelings. Thus John compares this love to a living flame that purifies and transforms and thereby makes us new. It cuts into the deepest core of our beings and renews us at the roots of our identity and our affections.

Rowan Williams in reference to John of the Cross notes that the work of God in our hearts often comes in the midst of the trials and challenges of daily life. He observes—following John of the Cross:

> Alienation and dread are produced by all kinds of experiences, by the frustrations and humiliations of daily life; for John himself, the hostility of his brothers and associates, the petty spite with which he as treated in his last months of life . . .[9]

But what anchors us, in our prayers and in the whole of our lives, is very specifically the knowledge of the love of God in Christ. Thus, from Ignatius, Teresa, and John, we learn that the encounter with the love of God in Christ is a transformative one. God in Christ is transforming us into the image of God as we are increasingly brought into union with Christ through the gracious work of the Spirit.

And from our personal experience and knowledge of the love of God, we move into the company of the people of God and heartily sing: "O the Deep Deep Love of Jesus, Vast, unmeasured, boundless and free."[10] And as we must stress when we speak of vocation and the ascension (in chapter 6), it is the love of God that compels us (2 Cor 5:14). We move from personal

---

7. Julian of Norwich, *Revelations of Divine Love* ¶7.
8. John of the Cross, *Living Flame of Love* ¶19.
9. Williams, *Silent Action*, 178.
10. "O the Deep Deep Love of Jesus," Samuel Trevor Francis.

Personal and Solitary Prayer

and solitary prayer into community and into service in the world, all sustained and motivated by the love of God in Christ for us. This knowledge is personal and particular. Each of us knows, through encounter with the ascended Lord, that we are loved.

What is critical in all of this is the affirmation that this cannot be choreographed. We do not manage the exchange with God. Our experience of the transcendence of God, in Christ, comes to us in God's timing and as God determines that we are ready and willing with open hearts to know the love of God and live in this love.

Thus we speak of solitude—the individual, solitary encounter with the benevolent God who is present to us in Christ, in whom and through whom we know the breadth and width of the love of God. We long to know the voice of Jesus—personally and in a way that equips and empowers for life and work: we long to discern the call of God on our lives. And the point is simply this, as John of the Cross stresses: "God speaks to the heart in . . . solitude . . . while the soul listens . . . to what the Lord God speaks to it (Ps 84:9), for He speaks this peace in this solitude."[11] The point, though, is that this is not just any solitude: it is the solitary encounter *with* Christ—the embodiment of the love of God, an encounter that is in itself an experience of the transforming grace of God. Yes, it is solitary, and in solitude we learn to be silent and attentive, but there is a "liturgy," a form by which we are drawn into the presence of the living and ascended Jesus.

Thus I stress that the Christian vision of solitary prayer—of the priority of solitude in the spiritual life—has three essential caveats: first it is the complement to shared and common worship; second, it has a focus—the benevolent and transforming grace of God in Christ, the ascended Lord; and third, it ultimately is about empowering us and equipping us for vocation in the world. And it is all three together. The common worship reflects our active participation in the community of faith and our own accountability to that community as a reflection of the historic Christian witness to the Triune God and the centrality of Christ. Our solitary prayers are not our own projection of Christ, but an encounter with the Christ who is worshipped in community with God's people. And then, our vocation in the world is not our own vision—a kind of messianic resolve to save the world—but rather a recognition of the perhaps unique contribution we will make alongside the gifts and talents of others, those very ones with whom we are in community. But we see and experience all of this as those who

---

11. John of the Cross, *Living Flame of Love* ¶34.

know what it means to be "alone with the Lord"—as those who know the grace that comes with solitude as an indispensable element of our lives as Christian believers.

Contemplation and Self-Knowledge

The encounter with the ascended Lord, in our prayers, is an encounter with the love of God, manifested to us in Christ. But more, this encounter fosters our capacity to not only see and know Christ, but also to know ourselves. We learn from the mystical tradition that this encounter with Christ fosters self-awareness and self-knowledge. In *The Spiritual Exercises* Ignatius graciously guides the pray-er towards a capacity to see oneself as God sees us: to be open and authentic and humbly present to God—no pretense or posturing. This is spoken of as the grace that we seek in the first week of the *Exercises*.

It is given more extensive treatment in Teresa. For Teresa, this self-knowledge is essential for wisdom, but more, it is essential for an authentic experience of prayer. Self-knowledge is humility; and, without humility, she insists, "everything goes wrong."[12] Or later, "Knowing ourselves is something so important that I wouldn't want any relaxation in this regard, however high you have climbed into the heavens."[13] With self knowledge we not only know ourselves but accept ourselves for who God made us to be; we are, to use contemporary parlance, "at peace in our own skin." What is noteworthy is that like Calvin in the opening of the *Institutes*, Teresa stresses that knowledge of ourselves and of our humanity is intimately linked to our knowledge of God: we only come to know God as we come to know ourselves; we only know ourselves as we come to know God.[14]

Teresa insists that our knowledge of God is profoundly interconnected with our self-knowledge, or, more specifically, that an encounter with the ascended Lord fosters our capacity to see ourselves in truth. In meeting Christ in our prayers we come to greater self-awareness of who we are. We grow in our capacity to "take a sober look at ourselves" (Rom 12:3). Solitude and a personal encounter with Christ lead not to narcissism or a preoccupation with self: the solitary encounter is one wherein we are freed from narcissism, freed from a self-centered posture, freed from being overly concerned with ourselves.

12. Teresa of Avila, *Interior Castle*, I, 2, ¶8.
13. Teresa of Avila, *Interior Castle*, I, 2, ¶9.
14. Teresa of Avila, *Interior Castle*, I, 2, ¶9.

Personal and Solitary Prayer

We must highlight something in this sequence: that we come to self-knowledge out of an encounter with the love of God, and thus the sober awareness of our strengths and limitations, of our victories and defeats, does not diminish or crush us. It is to the contrary liberating. Knowing in heart and mind that we are loved and that we dwell in the mercy of God frees us to engage our world with alacrity and courage.

More specifically, this knowledge of the love of God in Christ frees us towards a greater capacity to discern where and how we are being called to participate in the purposes of God in the world. In prayer we experience the transforming grace of God and we come to a greater awareness of where and how we are being called participate in the world of God who is creator and redeemer. In our prayers we come to see that we are not mere spectators to what God is doing in the world. Neither are we asking, what would Jesus do? Rather, we are discerning where and how God is present and active in our world and where and how we are called to participate in this work. Our encounter with the risen and ascended Christ actually brings us into the equation—not as mere spectators, but as those who through prayer are changed and who through prayer discern how we are called to be participants, with Christ, in and for the purposes of God in the world.

Thus we see that the encounter with the ascended Christ does not diminish the human person. Rather, a consciousness of the ascension profiles the potential for human flourishing and transformation, and further it gives weight to human agency—not as hero or diva or star actor in the drama, but nevertheless a full participant in the purposes of God, in the drama of God's redemptive activity in the world. More on this when we come to chapter 6 on the ascension and human vocation.

Contemplation and Calling: From Encounter to Engagement with Our World

There is more. From Ignatius in particular we come to see that our engagement with the world is the fruit of this encounter with Christ: we know the voice of Jesus who calls us and grants us clarity about what it means for us to be in the world.

Our encounter with Christ is not purely pragmatic; we do not go on retreat or into solitude merely to get our "marching orders," as my forefathers and mothers might have said. The first priority in this encounter is to know Christ and to love Christ more fully; and then and only then from that awareness do we then turn in anticipation of our movement into the world, seeking to know the call of God for our lives and the work to which we are called. For many pray-ers, this is the huge and specific value of the *Spiritual Exercises*: there is a pacing, a facing up to our interior selves that is essential part of sequence by which we come to clarity about God's call on our lives. We do not rush to a discernment question; we come by this slowly and surely even as we are growing in our capacity to live in the love of God.

But then, for sure, we do come to some clarity about this call: we hear the voice of Jesus. This call is personal and individual. It is not generic but specific. It is like the calling of Moses and his encounter with the burning bush, or the experience of Samuel when Eli keeps sending him back to his place of solitude, or the calling of the prophet Isaiah and his classic response, "here am I; send me" (Isa 7:8), or the response of Jonah to his call. Later, we have the call of Mary and her encounter with the angel Gabriel; and also, the calling of the original twelve disciples. Or the calling of Paul on the road to Damascus. Or a generation later we see reference to calling in the opening verses of the Second Letter to Timothy.

Some of these events are rather dramatic: Moses and the burning bush, for example, and Isaiah with the burning coal, and Mary with the visit from the angel Gabriel. And we might all wish we could have such a visit: when we are overwhelmed with all that needs to be done, an angel visiting us likely feels like the perfect antidote to the confusion we feel in our circumstances.[15] But for most Christians over the centuries the call of God has likely been more like of that of Elijah, who heard the call of God not in the earthquake or the wind or the fire, but in the sound of sheer silence (1 Kgs 19:11–12).

Can we hear this voice—the voice of Jesus in the quiet, in the stillness and in the silence? Or do we lead such busy and distracted lives that the voice of Jesus is drowned out by the noise all around us. Can our shared or common worship cultivate a sense of transcendence such that we can each, in the context of our personal prayers, know with conviction and clarity the call of God on our lives? Can we get beyond the craving for the dramatic and ecstatic and learn in the quietness of our daily lives and solitary prayers to attend to how the ascended Christ is calling us to speak and to act in our time and in our place?

15. I confess that I often hesitate a little when singing the hymn "Spirit of God, Descend Upon My Heart" and the line in the second verse, "I ask no dream, no prophet ecstasies . . . No angel visitant . . ." As we sing I think to myself, "Actually, an angel just about now would be very helpful!"

Personal and Solitary Prayer

The Ignatian spiritual tradition affirms that the counterpart to knowing Christ through contemplative prayer is the capacity to recognize and see that God is in the world and active in our world. We can know what it means to "find God in all things." It is not that we merely, to use the language of the Dominican tradition—language given currency by St. Thomas Aquinas—share the fruits of contemplation. We go into the world as those who pray, but we also come to our prayers as those who engage the world. For Ignatius, we actually encounter Christ in the world. Christ goes before us and our work in the world is a participation in what Christ is already doing in the world. And yet, we say this with a caveat: that we can only see how God is active in our world when and as we are attentive to the movement of our God in our own hearts. Our capacity to see where and how Christ is present in our world arises from or is derivative from the encounter with Christ in worship and prayer.

What all of this challenges is the misguided and simplistic call of many: that when someone is wrestling with a key matter in their lives, we simply advise them to "pray over it and God will show you the way," which is useless and simplistic advice if they have not learned the habits of heart and mind by which they can come to an awareness of the consolation in which they can discern a way forward. And most of all it all too easily appears mechanical, as though God is simply an answer machine rather than first and foremost the God in whose company we find our deep solace and a profound awareness that we are loved.

In discernment, two things guide our thinking and our prayers. First, as noted, we are grounded in an affective awareness of the love of God. And second, a vital dimension of the Ignatian vision is captured by the motto of so many Jesuit institutions, *ad majorem dei gloriam*—to the greater glory of God. This perspective or vision arises from the conviction that when all is said and done it is not about us, but about Christ and his reign. It is not about our reputation or comfort or power, but the glory of the ascended Christ. And the means to this end is that we know the grace of what is spoken of as "holy indifference," which speaks not of apathy but to a settledness of heart—a clarity of conviction about what it is that matters most. We forego wealth, fame, and influence. This is what makes discernment possible. We seek only the will of God in Christ. We set aside our own aspirations and desires eager that our lives would be lived to the glory of Christ. We are freed, to use the language of the *Exercises*, from inordinate attachments (notably: riches, honor, pride).¹⁶ We have peace to say "not my will, but thy will be done."

The centerpiece of our encounter with Christ is the grace of *consolation*—the peace or joy that can only be attributed to this encounter—what others have spoken of as the "consolation without previous cause." This is the consolation that can only be attributed to Christ himself and not to an earthly pleasure or catalyst. However, this needs to be stated with an important caveat: not every experience of consolation necessarily comes from God. Vital to the Ignatian vision of prayer is the recognition that evil enters into our lives and our prayers under the guise of the good—that "the evil one masquerades as an angel of light"(2 Cor 14).

We are so very capable of self-rationalizations. Thus true prayer is complemented by a growing capacity to *discern*—to confirm that what we are experiencing is truly from God. There is within this tradition a healthy self-suspicion. We do not assume or presume that positive or warm feelings necessarily mean that the Spirit is active in our lives. We pray knowing that we all have a capacity for self-deception and rationalizations. And yet, we are not so paralyzed by self-doubt that we cannot act. We can choose and choose in faith and a knowledge of the love and purposes of God for us. We can make basic choices, critical action items that shape our future and that of others. We can choose and do that which is necessary.

We long to choose well—with conviction, alacrity, and courage. What the Ignatian tradition gives us is a way forward: an approach to prayer by which we can come to a decision. And yet, discernment is only authentic and effective if it is part of the rhythm of our daily lives. We discern only as well as we live; we discern well in times of choice if and only if there is an attentiveness to the voice of Jesus in our daily experience.

What lies behind all of this is Teresa's emphasis that prayer is not an end in itself. Rather, the evidence of authentic contemplative prayer is generosity of service for one's neighbor, in the world.¹⁷ Contemplative prayer is not the prayer of escape from the world but rather it is the prayer of encounter with Christ through which we know the grace to be fully *present* to our world. This is an echo of what we find within the Ignatian tradition, the notion of "the contemplative in action." True prayer consists not, ultimately, in spiritual delight but in a life lived with greater love for others and deeds

---

16. Ignatius, *Spiritual Exercises*, ¶142.
17. Teresa of Avila, *Interior Castle*, ¶351.

done in truth and justice.[18] The signs of authentic and mature prayer, then, are these: inner confidence and peace and a life lived in generous service for others. External engagement arises from that inner peace that frees us and empowers us to do what needs to be done. Teresa addresses how we might be tempted to do grandiose things—what she speaks of as "great desires." But she counsels that we need to be content with the immediate requirement that Christ has set before us.[19]

Without contemplation we are casting about, busy in the world but in many respects flailing—hoping to do good work that is aligned with Christ's kingdom purposes, but it is hit and miss. As such, worship and contemplative prayer are the essential counterparts to missional engagement. When our work in the world is all busyness and frenetic or anxious engagement, or when in our personal lives we feel overwhelmed with all that needs to be done or we have lost a sense of perspective, the imperative is the realignment that comes with the prayer of contemplative engagement with Christ.

Contrary to the stereotype that contemplatives are so heavenly minded that they are of no earthly good, the truth of the matter is that we are only of earthly good if we are heavenly minded. The contemplative is much more fruitful in the kingdom purposes of God in the world than the activist.

In my growing up there was a song that we loved to sing: "Turn your eyes upon Jesus; look full in his wonderful face; and the things of earth will grow strangely dim, in the light of his glory and grace."[20] While I get the intent of the song, I wonder if Ignatius would suggest otherwise: that when we see Jesus—the ascended Christ—the things of earth come to greater clarity. We see ourselves and our circumstances more truthfully and accurately; we have a better and more nuanced appreciation of the challenges that we are facing. Rather than dimness we have clarity. Contemplatives see both themselves and the world more clearly. Very specifically, they have insight into themselves and their world that is informed by the real-time encounter with Christ.

Thus worship leads to work, liturgy to labor. We worship and pray as those who are in the world, but crucially, we are in the world as those who have seen the Lord. That is, appreciating the force of the call to prayer in

18. Teresa of Avila, *Interior Castle*, ¶313.

19. Teresa of Avila, *Interior Castle*, ¶¶449–50.

20. "Turn Your Eyes Upon Jesus," also known as "The Heavenly Vision," by Helen Howarth Lemmel.

Hebrews 4:14–16, that we come to prayer before the ascended Christ out of our "time of need." In both our worship and in our solitary prayers we come into the presence of Christ as those who have been in the world and felt the full force of the fragmentation and need of our world. And then we return to the world, specifically to the work to which we have been called, as those who have met Christ and received his grace for our time of need (Heb 4:16).

Contemplation and the Dark Night

All of this assumes—though it is more evident in Teresa and then perhaps most of all in John of the Cross—that we can and must mature in our prayers. At first, we are beginners, eager to know God and the blessings and benefits of knowing God. The crucial shift in our prayers comes when we become less and less aware of ourselves and more and more aware of God and, specifically, the love of God. Self-knowledge is essential to this journey, but one of the key indicators that we are maturing in our prayers is that we become less and less self-absorbed and more and more aware of the love of God in Christ Jesus.[21] We move from thinking much to loving much—which may seem an awkward way of stating it, but in many respects this captures what Teresa is stressing—notably in the Fourth Mansion, when we come to that point in the journey where our deepest joy is God and not merely the gifts of God.

Within my own theological and spiritual tradition, this sentiment is captured by a hymn by the founder of the denomination,[22] A. B. Simpson, when he has us sing:

> Once it was the blessing, now it is the Lord;
> Once it was the feeling, now it is His Word;
> Once the gift I wanted, now the Giver own,
> Once I sought for healing, now himself alone.

I am sure that colleagues and friends within the denomination would agree that this hymn is virtually unsingable and thus we would not foist it on others! But the sentiments capture precisely the genius of the mystical tradition as articulated by Teresa and John of the Cross.

---

21. Teresa of Avila, *Interior Castle*, ¶¶311–13.
22. The Christian and Missionary Alliance.

Personal and Solitary Prayer

The challenge, of course, is that we long for the *felt* awareness of God—for John in the sixteenth century but even more so now. We are part of religious communities that assume that the more powerful the positive feelings in worship and prayer, the greater the evidence that God is present. So worship leaders manipulate the heartstrings to create a sense of warm feelings on the assumption that if it feels good, it is a transformative experience—an encounter with the ineffable. But Teresa and John press their readers to appreciate that feelings and especially the craving for ecstatic feelings can be a profound distraction to the authentic experience of prayer and transformative encounter with God.

Rowan Williams, in his reflections on the wisdom of John of the Cross, observes that "the life of the heart is not in the ecstatic or the extraordinary . . ." And further, again citing Williams, "no 'spiritual' experience whatsoever can provide a clear security, an unambiguous sign of God's favour." And this means that while "experiences of wordless intensity and certainty must be accepted," they are "not to be desired or relied upon . . ."[23]

What it all comes down to is simply this: in this life, we never get beyond our identification with the crucified and immolated lamb. We never get beyond the awareness of the power and grace of the suffering with and for Christ. This means that we must live with an inevitable ambiguity in life and work and ministry. Our worship is marked by both praise and lament. Our work in the world necessarily includes success and blessing as well as failure and setbacks. More needs to be said on this score when we speak of the ascension and the mission of the church—in the upcoming chapter 5.

The north star that guides us through all the points of confusion and uncertainty in our lives and work, through trial and difficulty as well as times of success and blessing, is the love of God. This knowledge of the love of God is personal and profound; it defines us like nothing else. Thus Ignatius of Loyola in the *Spiritual Exercises* invites us to into a "Contemplation of the Love of God." And John of the Cross just as insistently calls us to a knowledge of the love of God while he reminds us that this knowledge is not to be reduced to nice feelings. Yet the bottom line remains: we live here; we abide here; this is our true home. And in our prayers—week in and week out—we cultivate a dynamic and liberating awareness of this love—given to us as a gift of the Spirit (Rom 5:5) and in fulfillment of the call of the apostle that we would know the "breadth and length and height and depth . . . the love of Christ that surprises knowledge" (Eph 3:18-19). To this end, we

---

23. Williams, *Wound of Knowledge*, 173.

In the Meantime

lean into the witness of the sixteenth-century Spanish reformers and spiritual writers who stress that this is a grace available to all Christians.

This is the grace we seek in the midst of the vicissitudes of life and work: to know Jesus more fully, love him more deeply, and then turn and serve him more generously. We move from prayer to engagement, from prayer to work and our vocations in the world. Our personal prayer, the complement to the liturgy of the church—our common prayer with God's people—reflects a desire for and encounter with the ascended Christ who then calls us into his service. Thus we fulfill our vocations as those who have met Christ in real time.

5

Christian Mission in the Meantime

TOGETHER, AS THE CHURCH—AS the people of God—we are eagerly engaged in the mission of God in the world. And together, we are engaged in this mission in the meantime, between the ascension and the second coming, between the *already* of the kingdom—Christ is ascended—and the not yet—the fullness of the kingdom that is yet to come.

When it comes to the mission of the church in the world, there tend to be two ways in which this has been and envisioned and engaged—two perspectives that tend to dominate the conversation and the ways in which the mission of the church in the world is framed.

Mission When the Kingdom Is *Future* Tense

The first, for those of us who grew up evangelical, mission is stated simply and entirely in terms of the kingdom that is yet to come. Mission is all about doing what needs to be done *now* so we are ready for the next world. The kingdom of God is future and all we do now is what is necessary and appropriate if not actually urgent. Mission is about saving souls not for this life but for the life that is yet to come. Evangelism is all about urging others to get their personal affairs in order, so that at the consummation of the kingdom their eternal destiny is set.

In the Meantime

Any reference to the past when it comes to mission was typically referring to the place of the cross in mission: Christ died for you (past tense) and if you accept and choose to live in this reality your future (in heaven) is secure. In this perspective, mission is all about speaking this "gospel" so that people will go to heaven. This is the good news—that "Christ died for you and you too can go to heaven." "Heaven," of course, is shorthand for the *future* kingdom of God—the kingdom that is yet to come.

It is a definition of mission that makes little or no reference at all to the fact that Christ is now ascended and now sits on the throne and that the kingdom of God has come. And thus, one major shortfall of this vision for the mission of the church was that it took no account of what it means to live out the Christian life now—in the present—in this world. Thus we have what Richard Lovelace spoke of as the "sanctification gap"—basically no vision for or capacity for spiritual formation and nurture, what we might also speak of as "Christian discipleship" in this life.[1] There were those who recognized a problem and there is within the evangelical Christian community a growing insistence on the need for cultivating mature disciples. And yet, the gap remains.

Church leadership can decry the lack of discipleship and maturity in Christians but the lack naturally follows from this understanding of mission. It is the inevitable result of a truncated understanding of the mission of God. When you have this vision of mission, you will not likely have a vigorous practice of disciple-making.

I grew up in this world and my parents were part of a generation of Christian missionaries who assumed, as part of their denomination and mission agency, that one should sacrifice everything for the sake of the gospel and getting souls saved, even if this meant sending your children to a missionary children boarding school. These schools had problems, though these paled in comparison with the residential schools that were part of the experience of the Indigenous people of Canada and elsewhere. While I am grateful for those children and young people who flourished in these schools, I know too many adults—peers to myself and my children—for whom this separation from parents was traumatic. And so, I am deeply grateful to my parents who saw the light and defied mission authorities and insisted that I would live with them and go to a local school in Guayaquil, Ecuador.

My parents did not use the language of the ascension or the language of the "already" and "not yet." But they knew that their witness for God and

---

1. Lovelace, *Dynamics of Spiritual Life*, 229–37.

for the reign of God in Christ of necessity meant that they were living out their faith as a family, as parents, as an essential and integral dimension of their Christian witness.

But here is the main point: this vision of the mission of God in the world leads to a faulty vision of the Christian life and a failure to articulate an understanding of maturity in Christ in response to the reality of the ascension—that, indeed, the kingdom of God is at hand and that we live *now* in the fullness of this extraordinary reality.

Mission When the Kingdom Is *Present* Tense

The second approach to mission is in some ways the reverse or inverse of the first. Rather than the kingdom being in the future, it is now: today and immediate. *We* bring about the kingdom. The assumption is that there is such a thing as a Christian nation that today can embody the kingdom of God: a nation that while perhaps is spoken of as a foretaste of what is yet to come, is lived out as though it is both possible and desirable to establish a nation-state where the Christian faith is dominant—if not officially and legally, in effect it is a country where this is the only religious option.

Even where the Christian religion is not officially the faith of the nation, this approach to mission assumes that "Christian" principles—moral and theological—are written (or should be) into the laws and statues of the nation-state. Much has been made of how the United States of America was established on the principle that church and state are inherently separate. The idea was that this would be in contrast to European models of government and church. The US constitution was written as an intentional contrast to the European pattern: in the US church and state would be distinct and no religion would have the imprimatur of the state. But in reality, a whole segment of the United States population assume that when you vote, you want to support a political party that will keep America "Christian," on the assumption that the US is a Christian nation.

In this case, the mission of the church is highly politicized. Through active work at the ballot box, in legislatures, and in the courts, there is an ongoing and systematic attempt to keep the church deeply embedded within the state, able to shape legislation that is aligned with what are spoken of as Christian values. Often the language of "biblical" is used as a kind of litmus test of authentic religion: true Christianity is "biblical," "conservative," and, in some quarters, "fundamentalist." High-profile religious leaders give their blessing to politicians who will align public and civic policy and legislation with what those religious leaders view as making the nation more Christian.

In Catholic circles, the language is a little different—but the assumptions are the same. Catholic integralism, for example, insists that ultimately Catholic ideological and moral understanding needs to be the basis for the state and for the laws of the land. And this assumes a rejection of both religious pluralism or the idea that Catholics are neutral towards civic authorities.

In the first vision of mission, the kingdom is future; in the second, the kingdom is now—today and immediate—typically in a state that either claims to be Christian or at least idealizes the national past as though it were Christian. The battleground for the first is the other religious systems of the world; for the second, the focus is on the legislatures, the courts, and the schools, since each has a formative influence within a society. And it is assumed, in both visions actually, that if you have enough money and political influence you can achieve your intended outcomes. War language is used in both schemes: "Onward Christian Soldiers" might be sung and the assumption is that Christians are called into a great spiritual battle against the forces of darkness and evil. For the first vision of mission, other religions are inherently demonic; for the second, any resistance to the agenda of Christian nationalism is denounced as a threat to the purposes of God in the world. Typically, Christian nationalists support more ideologically right-wing governments and demonize anyone from the political "left."

There is a song that reflects this vision of mission that is often sung in evangelical Christian circles, where after singing "build your kingdom . . ." one then sings "win this nation back," on the assumption, presumably, that the kingdom and the nation are one and the same.[2] When I served as the president of a Christian university, I was struck by how in our chapel gatherings the students so enjoyed this song and sang it with great gusto. However, the language of "build the kingdom" is not New Testament language. The New Testament speaks of entering the kingdom and of the kingdom as something to which we witness or testify; we learn to live the light of the kingdom that is described as a relationship with the one who sits on the throne.

We enter into the kingdom with the disposition of children—with humility and openheartedness. And then the defining line of the song: "heal our streets and land . . . win this nation back." This could be a theme

---

2. "Build Your Kingdom Here," by Chris Llewellyn, Gareth Gilkeson, and Will Heron.

song for Christian nationalism or Catholic integralism—where the nation becomes the kingdom.[3]

And so we have two very different perspectives on the mission of the church. In the first, the salvation of God is all future; and in the second, salvation amounts to establishing the kingdom here and now in our own nation-states. For both it is interesting to ask: what is the role of business and commerce in the mission of God? For the first, business is a way to open up points of entry and contact. Thus, for example, in countries that do not allow for a foreign missionary to proselytize, a business person can perhaps get a visa. This is typically spoken of as one's "cover." But the only reason for that business leader to do business in that country is to be a witness for the Christian faith and find opportunities to evangelize. Business in itself has little if any inherent value.

For the second vision of mission, business and commerce are about making sure that the nation-state is economically powerful and thus able to finance its agenda and priorities. In both cases, wealthy business leaders are assumed to be key voices and bring with them points of leverage—whether they are funding missionary endeavors or are supporting the agenda of a particular political party. And if they bring sufficient wealth to the civic square they can have direct influence on policy. I am thinking of the Amway conglomerate and Betsy DeVos, who was secretary of education in the US with literally no qualifications for the role other than that she was a major financial supporter of Donald Trump's electoral campaign.

What is of particular interest is that both perspectives on the kingdom assume a level of human agency—that with the right alignment of power and money we can bring about the kingdom. In short, we can make it happen. We can lay out a vision of an intended future—and with a plan of action, and the leveraging of resources, we can deliver the kingdom of God. We can be heroes; we can deliver results.

In the first perspective, foreign missionaries are spoken of as having the anointing of God—they are the heroes, the agents of the kingdom. In the second perspective, it is political leaders who speak of being anointed, for they are the agents that bring about the kingdom. They are those who make a difference for God and for the kingdom of God. Both understandings are deeply pragmatic: the means justify the ends. Thus the Catholic

---

3. Few have written to powerfully about the huge compromise that this entails as Jaques Ellul. While much of Ellul's message can be found a half-century earlier in Søren Kierkegaard, I remain impressed by Ellul's critique of the Reformed Protestant Church in France; see especially his *False Presence of the Kingdom*.

Church will support the authoritarian leadership of Ferdinand Marcos in the Philippines. And in Christian nationalism, one justifies support for a morally compromised political leader—a pathological liar, racist, misogynist, authoritarian—on the assumption that this person can help make the nation more "Christian." Violence is even justified, if it can, as it is thought, make America Christian again. This is no different than the blessing of the Catholic Church on the Spanish and Portuguese conquistadors of the seventeenth century.

What we can and need to see is that both of these perspectives on mission are deeply problematic: they represent, at best, half-truths. Fundamentally, neither takes adequate account of the meaning and significance of the ascension and thus the already and the not-yet of the kingdom of God.

Mission in Light of the Ascension

Is there another way to think of the mission of the church in the world that avoids these pitfalls? More to the point, what are the implications of the ascension for how we think about mission and how we engage the world in which we live and are called to be witnesses to the reign of Christ? What does the ascension mean for those of us who long to be full participants in the kingdom purposes of God in the world and in the cosmos? What does it mean, in other words, that Christ *does* reign on the throne of the universe; that Jesus announced that the kingdom of God was at hand; and we know that it has come with the ascension? And yet, what we also know is that the kingdom has not yet come in fullness.

The mission of God and of the church in the world is fulfilled precisely in this dynamic—this liminal space, between the "already" of the kingdom and the "not yet" of the kingdom of God. What does it mean to participate in the mission of God in the meantime? I offer three observations that might provide us with a way to engage the mission of God in the world in the meantime, in intentional alignment with the vision and mission of the ascended Christ.

Our Lives and Our Work in this World Have Inherent Value and Worth

First, the ascension means that our lives matter. Our work today—in this time and place—has significance rather than assuming that the only thing that counts is the kingdom to come. Or where the only legitimate work is getting conversions and the arts and business only have value insofar as they support making converts. With the ascension and the affirmation that the kingdom of God has come, we can and must fully affirm the vital calling and place of those called into the arts, into education, and into business. Are there more vocations? Yes, of course there are. But there is a sense in which we only get it—the ascension—when we affirm these three spheres of activity in the world. These three are good indicators that we know that this world matters and matters to God. Indeed, in the missional purposes of God, especially in a post-Christian and secular context, the arts, education, and business may well have *more* weight and significance than pioneer evangelism. What we come to see is that believers live out a kingdom way of being in the workplace as living and embodied witnesses to the reign of God. And they do so in the here and now.

Further, it means that all signs and indictors of human flourishing are reason for celebration and thanksgiving. We affirm and celebrate truth and goodness and the triumph of grace wherever and whenever they appear, whether the artist or the philosopher or the businessperson is a Christian or not. Where there is truth and goodness in another religious persuasion, we do not demonize but give thanks; where a business is doing good work—respecting and honoring their suppliers and generously serving their customers and treating their employees honorably—we give thanks, whether they are explicitly Christian or not.

It means that we care for this earth: the kingdom of God is at hand; Christ reigns *now*, on this earth. And so we tend to the land and learn to care for the garden in which we have been placed as stewards of God's created order. We celebrate the beauty and wonder of the creation and tend to its well-being rather than exploit it for selfish or greedy purposes. Environmental stewardship is an integral dimension of the mission of the church in the world.

It means that we pursue justice and mercy and walk humbly in our civic spaces. We do not demonize our political opponents but rather seek to learn *with* them and *from* them; and together we refuse to politicize matters of justice but rather see that now, with the kingdom of God at hand, we will and must seek a just social fabric that includes care for those at the margins. We read the Old Testament prophets as *our* prophets—as witnesses to *our* age and *our* time. They foretold the one who was yet to come, the Messiah, and signaled what it means to live under the authority and reign of this

Messiah. And as something central to the mission of church in the world, we seek peace with justice: we are agents of reconciliation. The pursuit of justice and peace between peoples at war is also equally integral to any verbal witness we might give to the gospel.

We advocate for those at the margins as something essential to our kingdom witness. We seek reconciliation with Indigenous peoples if we are settlers; we offer radical hospitality to the refugee and the immigrant. And we refuse to politicize either of these as the agenda of either the political left or right. Rather, we view such a way of being as nothing but a reflection of the call of the Old Testament prophets. The reality of the ascension gives meaning to our daily lives, including our advocacy for the just treatment of the creation and of all peoples.

And in the midst of it all, we plant a rose garden, or refill the birdfeeder on the veranda, or read a novel. And we keep a sense of humor. We observe sabbath rest—perhaps the ultimate declaration that we know that Christ is ascended and that therefore we can relax and rest and do not need to be perpetually active and productive. We can be present to the world and to the earth. We can delight in God's creation and enjoy the company of friends. We can resist the temptation to frenetic busyness and hectic activity.

And Yet, We Sing the Blues

Yes, the kingdom has come; but it has not yet come in fullness. Yes, we celebrate any indication of goodness and grace, the triumph of justice and any indication of the healing of creation.

And yet, and yet, we live in a deeply fragmented and broken world. And thus we face two rather different temptations at one and the same time. On the one hand we have those for whom the kingdom of God has come, and they seem blind to the fragmentation of our world. And on the other hand, we have those who see all the brokenness around us and despair that healing and wholeness and reconciliation can happen.

We can speak of the one temptation as pseudo-optimism, by which I mean the denial of the pain all around us. It is the temptation to overspeak or overstate the possibilities of grace: to speak of healing and wholeness and peace, but it is a peace that is superficial at best or perhaps only tangential and temporary—not a real engagement with the evil in our world and thus without any genuine lament for all that is so very wrong.

Christian Mission in the Meantime

But then for some, in the face of evil and wrong and fragmentation and brokenness, we can wonder if there is any genuine possibility of grace. Is any measure of hope merely a naïve optimism that is not naming reality and acknowledging the wrong? For some, the only credible option is to despair.

And it is to this that we must speak when we consider the mission of the church in the world between the ascension and the consummation of the kingdom. Can we live and work as those who are fully engaged with this world, with all that is so very wrong? And can we accept that we live in a troubled world without losing hope? Can we be patient and let God do God's work in God's time and thus graciously and humbly live with the less than perfect? Without despair?

Can we do what we are called to do—exercising vision and talent, with both courage and wisdom—but also recognize the limits of human agency? Can we be invested in the purposes of God in the world but recognize that we are *not* in control of our destinies? Can we appreciate that we are *not* masters of our futures; we are *not* able to shape the countries, entities, agencies, and churches to our preferred outcome? We plant, yes; we water, of course. But the results are in the hands of God, as Paul makes so clear (in 1 Cor 3:6–8).[4]

So much strategic planning—in churches, nonprofits, and even mission organizations—assumes that we can make things happen. We can identify a preferred future, and we can leverage time, human energy, actions, and resources so as to reach this goal or this ideal outcome. We can make our preferred future the *actual* future.

In similar fashion, there is this narrative within our faith communities that suggests that we can choreograph the spiritual lives of our children so that they grow up to be the ideal we have for them. We can identify the preferred outcome for our church and with the right plans in place, we can deliver. Through strategic planning we can be masters of our destinies.

However, what the vision of the already and the not-yet tells us is that we have influence but very little control. We can make a difference, but we can only see as far as the next bend in the road. In our lives, there are so many variables over which we have little say or control, but that affect our future. Our lives and our work are in a state of constant improvisation—learning to adapt and respond in light of what is actually the case

---

4. I chuckle as I write this, in that this was the constant message of my spiritual director for may years—Father Thomas Ryan—who I suspect feared that he was making little progress with someone like myself so much a part of an activist religious subculture. But he said it again and again: "We do our work, Gordon, and leave the results to God."

and what God is actually doing in our world. We have plans and intentions, but then life, specifically the messiness of life, interrupts and forces us to adjust, adapt, rethink, and innovate. We do not control outcomes; we do not choreograph the kingdom.

This is never an excuse for incompetence or laziness or mediocrity! Rather, recognizing this puts our talent and efforts in perspective. We learn to simply do what we are called to do—no more and no less—without frenetic busyness or anxiety. We cannot control our destinies or desired outcomes. Having said that, it is important to note that, actually, we do get things done: we prepare a meal, and build a house and write a book, teach a class, preach a sermon and complete a painting. Stuff does get done; we do have signs and indicators of the kingdom that has come. My point is merely that we cannot choreograph our future or that of our families, our institutions, or our churches. We live in the midst of messy, complex, and far-from-ideal circumstances. Living with grace—with hope, patience, and alacrity, even in the midst of all this uncertainty—is surely at least part of what it means to live in light of the ascension.

You may be a brilliant therapist, but you know full well that while you *can* make a difference, there are so many variables outside of your control that your client may well descend into addiction and darkness, through no fault of your own. It is merely that we recognize the limits of human agency.

This is why we plant a rose garden. We witness to the staggering beauty of God's creation but also chuckle each time a thorn catches us unawares, reminding us not so very subtly that the kingdom of God is also "not yet." And we sing the blues. These are the hymns of those who understand that while we live in a broken and fragmented world, we will not despair: I think of the haunting line from Bruce Cockburn in "Waiting for a Miracle," when he cries, "Why does history take such a long, long time?"

We will sing "my mother told me there would be days like this" and yet not give up hope: we name our reality but we are still singing. Whether it is Van Morrison and his "Days Like This"—coming out of the experience of the Northern Ireland—or the African American journey from the racism of the Deep South to some measure of health and even joy, all of us can learn to sing the blues. Every day there will be a reminder that we have not yet arrived, the kingdom of God has not come in fullness, and yet we will sing and sustain a resilient hope and encourage one another on the road.

We will not despair but do our work—what we are called to do—in a way that is faithful to the task at hand. And this often means that we lead and work and witness to the reign of Christ in times of uncertainty, transition, and fragmentation. Such were the times of one of the most significant political players in American history: Abraham Lincoln. In his comprehensive and insightful overview of the life and influence of Lincoln, Jon Meacham makes a series of observations that are insightful. Lincoln was an extraordinary figure, no doubt; but he was also a flawed individual—a man of both virtue and vice—a man who despite all his limitations managed to be a force for positive change just when the world in which he lived and worked verged on chaos and deep fragmentation. As Meacham notes, "Lincoln kept America's democratic project alive."[5]

He stresses that Lincoln was not alone; many others were essential to the preservation of the union that was and is the United States of America. But, he writes, "Lincoln was essential in his moral vision for an America free of slavery." Again, not because he was perfect but because in a profoundly complex and messy and convoluted political environment he moved the dial. Meacham writes:

> Abraham Lincoln did not bring about heaven on earth. Yet he defended the possibilities of democracy and the pursuit of justice at an hour in which the means of amendment, adjustment and reform were under assault. His moral and political vision was to bring "a flawed nation closer to the light."[6]

The question then is this: when we participate in the mission of the ascended Christ, can we sustain a similar resilience? As women and men of principle and conviction, can we bring our own institutions and communities "closer to the light"? Can we be stewards of the opportunities and talents that God has given us to witness to the reign of Christ in the world?

To this end, we will read and reread the Russians—notably Tolstoy and Dostoevsky. We will be present at the theater for Shakespeare's *King Lear* and *Macbeth*. We will be at the concert hall for Rachmaninov's *Vespers* or Beethoven's string quartets. We will let the arts do their essential part. If the artists and composers are honest, there is no kitsch; no mere sentimentality. This is the key to this posture of life. We feel the full force of the fragmentation of his world. We lament. And yet, we do not despair. We do not give up. This is what it means to live in the meantime. With the ascension we choose to set our minds on things above, confident that evil

---

5. Meacham, *And There Was Light*, 418.
6. Meacham, *And There Was Light*, 419.

will not have the last word and that the goodness of God will triumph in due time. We will look to Jesus, the author and perfecter of our faith. We will gather with the people of God week in and week out to affirm together, with resolve and conviction, that the reign of Christ has come and that in the end Christ will reign. We will allow worship to do its magic: sustaining for us a vision of the ascended Lord.

With the Ascension We Need to Talk about the Church

Christ is establishing his reign, his kingdom; and our primary orientation or vision is toward the kingdom of God. We seek first the kingdom. What then of the church? In using the language of "church" it is important to stress that in what follows my use of this word refers not so much to denominations or denominational structures or denominational leadership, but rather to the church local: the gathering of the people of God within a time and place. It is a word that speaks of the community of faith in a particular geographic location.

This is perhaps the defining question in mission thinking today. While the kingdom and the church are not synonymous, we cannot have the one without the other: Christ is establishing his reign and, to that end, he is forming for himself a people. And thus, the mission of God is deeply ecclesial—it is a *churchly* endeavor. Very specifically it is faith communities that are the focus of mission—what in my tradition is spoken of as "church planting": congregations that are themselves, then, a living and embodied witness to the kingdom. Mission is not fundamentally about "saving souls" but about establishing communities of faith that in turn are about proclaiming and living in the realty of the salvation of God—precisely the kinds of spaces and places where people are coming to faith in Christ.

And further, mission is not fundamentally about establishing the kingdom of God on the earth through the political and civic structures of a society; it is about cultivating communities of faith that are a dynamic witness to the kingdom. This does not mean that saving souls is not essential to mission; it does not mean that civic engagement is irrelevant. It is, rather, that both of these are derivative of the primary focus: the local assembly of God's people who together, as a kingdom community, embody and witness to the reign of Christ in their lives and in the world. Here is where so many of us are indebted to the contribution of Lesslie Newbigin. In many respects it is Newbigin who has given us this perspective and language: that the church is "the living hermeneutic of the message of the Kingdom which it preaches."[7] So the church is a means to an end: witnessing to the reign of God in Christ.

And so we ask: what does mean for the church—the community of faith—to be a sign of the kingdom and as such a living and embodied witness to the ascended Lord? At the very least, it means three things—well, three and then a fourth element, hospitality, that informs all three.

First, these are communities of faith where worship happens—specifically worship that orients heart and mind into the presence of the ascended Lord. The church is first and foremost a worshipping community wherein those who lead worship bring us into a real-time encounter with the ascended Christ. Worship is not in essence an encounter with the Bible, but rather with the one who is revealed to us through the Scriptures; the Lord's Supper is not primarily an act of remembering what Christ has done for us; it is a real-time encounter with the risen and ascended Lord.

Second, these are communities of faith that are teaching/learning communities where the focus of the teaching is the reign of God in Christ and what it means to live and work in light of the kingdom. This teaching echoes the teaching of Jesus with the recurring and reverberating phrase, "the kingdom of God is like . . ." Communities of teaching and learning, disciple-making, are thus about equipping one and all to live in the world with minds and hearts set above, on the ascended Christ. We teach and preach the whole of the Scriptures, but give special place to the Beatitudes and the parables of Jesus, all of which form us with a way of thinking and being that reflects the reign of God in Christ.

Thus, for example, the Sermon on the Mount, the foundational teaching of Jesus in the Gospel of Mathew, is very specifically a call to live in the light of the kingdom of God. The sermon is a living embodiment of what it means to live and work and witness in this new reality, that Christ is ascended and the kingdom is at hand.

And yet, the kingdom has not yet come in fullness; and on this Jesus is also quite clear, if not explicit. And so, the parable of the wheat and the weeds (Matt 13) provides a glimpse into what it means to live and work and witness in this in-between and liminal time. The weeds are not to be pulled out; rather, the farmer needed to learn to live with a less than perfect harvest.

And then thirdly, these worshipping communities and teaching/ learning communities are also communities that empower and equip God's

---

7. Newbigin, *Sign of the Kingdom*, 43.

people to be in but not of the world, living as exiles who seek the peace of the city. They are faith communities that empower women and men, even as exiles within their social and cultural contest, to do business, to practice the arts, to participate in education, including public education—elementary, secondary, and higher education—all to witness in word and deed, in the marketplace, in schools, and in art galleries, to the reign of God. And we stop speaking of "mission" as something that only happens in foreign countries: all God's people are on mission, equipped and empowered by the church for the work to which they are called.

This means that preachers are announcing the kingdom of God while business leaders and artists and teachers are in the world providing a living and essential example of what we mean by the kingdom and what it means to live in light of the ascension. We preach it Sunday morning and we live it out on Monday morning. Yes, we do form and tend to the church local—faith communities that are marked by a vision for worship, teaching-learning, and mission. But what we come to see is that those called into business, education, and the arts play as crucial a role in mission today as those called into vocational religious leadership.

And those called into vocational Christian ministry are, essentially, called into the work of cultivating Christian communities. They assure that worship happens; they confirm that teaching and learning the way of the kingdom marks our common life; and they are skilled in equipping God's people to be all that they are called to be in the world.

The Lord of Mission, the Grace of the Lord, and the Presence of the Lord

In all of this, Christ is with us. It is not that Jesus went away and left others in charge on the assumption that it is now up to us to deliver on the kingdom. Christ is the Lord of the church and the Lord of the cosmos and is the one by whom and through whom all things are being reconciled to the Father. In that mission, there is only one hero and that is Christ himself.

Thus we can and must ask: with our focus on Christ, how and in what ways is the Spirit present and active in our world, at this time and in this place? The church lives by an intentional response to her Lord, attentive to the presence and work of the Spirit. Thus we read that the church in Antioch was in worship when it attended to the Spirit who called it to commission those who would be heading to Asia Minor (Acts 13:1–4). Those who went—Paul and Barnabas—then made the case in Jerusalem that gentile followers of Christ did not need to fulfill Jewish expectations to be full participants in the reign of Christ. Christ Jesus was doing a new thing, and the imperative was that the church recognize this new thing and respond accordingly. Thus there was no nostalgia—no looking back to the supposed good old days. Rather, we ask: what is Christ doing *today*, in our time and in our place? And we respond accordingly.

We can ask this question on a global scale and in the local context: in our own cities, towns, and neighborhoods.

And then also, we can and must note that we will regularly feel like we are in over our heads; our work and our lives matter and we can make a difference for good, but it is too much for us. And thus we lean into the grace of God again and again and again.

The good news is that Christ Jesus is not only the Lord of the cosmos and the church but also our high priest, and thus we come back often to the words of Hebrews 4 and the reminder that in our hour of perplexity and need, there is grace and grace abundant. Jesus, the Son of God, has passed through the heavens and as our priest is one to whom we can turn—the text even says we can approach the throne of grace with "boldness," "so that we may receive mercy and find grace to help in our time of need" (Heb 4:14–16).

We go into the world as worshippers—from the encounter with Christ to the engagement with our world; and then we come back to worship week in and week out and bring the sorrows and cares and needs of our world to the throne of grace. And thus "the prayers of the people" are a vital and essential element in our shared worship: our prayers reflect our engagement with the world. We go into the world as those who have been in worship; we come to worship as those who have been in the world and felt the fragmentation of the world in our own hearts. And this then informs our prayers.

And then we return to the world, from worship, with grace to participate in the mission of God in the meantime—in the liminal space between the ascension and the return of Christ. And in our worship and the prayers of the people we remind ourselves afresh of the promise of Christ, given just prior to the ascension, the concluding words of the Gospel of Matthew: "And remember, I am with you always, to the end of the age" (Matt 28:20).

The presence of Christ is powerful and immediate: he is with us, to the end. So yes, this is a time of much ambiguity, since we reject both pseudo-optimism and despair. It is not all black and white. We are not in control of our destinies. So then, how do we live with grace and sanity and even joy as we participate in the mission of the ascended Christ in the world? By being fully present to the one who says to us that he is with us always, to the end.

Hospitality as Basic Spiritual Practice

The bottom line is that the Christian community—the church—is the presence of Christ in the world: the embodiment of the ascended Lord. As such, this community, called to be in but not of the world, functions with a basic spiritual practice at the heart of its life and witness: hospitality. This suggests a compelling hospitality: toward one another, but also toward the society in which the faith community is located. It is always both/and. This hospitality then becomes one of the key indicators that the reign of God has come and will come and that in the meantime we will be a living embodiment of the reign of God in Christ. As a community, Christians welcome one another as Christ has welcomed them (Rom 15:7); this then is matched by their hospitality towards the world. What marks a church that is living in the light of the ascension is not a posture of judgment towards culture and the world, but a posture of generous hospitality. The faith community knows what means to welcome those who might feel diminished or shamed or despised by the world. They are the arms and the open heart of Jesus himself, the ascended Lord who is the living evidence of the wideness of God's mercy. And thus the church sings:

> There's a wideness in God's mercy, Like the wideness of the sea;
> There's a kindness in His justice, Which is more than liberty.
> There is welcome for the sinner, And more graces for the good;
> There is mercy with the Savior; There is healing in His blood.[8]

---

8. "Theres a Wideness in God's Mercy," by Frederick W. Faber.

6

Vocation and Work in the Meantime

WE NEED TO SPEAK to what it means to do our work—to fulfill a vocation, a calling in the world—in light of the ascension. From worship we move to mission. But then also, from our personal prayers—our solitary encounter with the ascended Christ—we embrace and engage the call of God on our own lives. We ask what the ascension means for vocation, work, and career; we consider what it means to do the work to which we are called, in the meantime. And the assumption here is that our work in the world is in response to the particular calling of Christ: specific and personal. We each hear this call—the invitation to *participate*, in word and deed, in the mission of Christ in the church and in the world.

And that word says it all: we participate. The remarkable dynamic that shapes our lives and gives meaning to our work is that we are invited to share in the work of the ascended Christ. We are not merely observers of the work of God in the world. The creator and redeemer of all things invites us into the drama of redemption. Christ is always the lead actor; we are not heroes or messiahs. But our work matters and it makes a difference.

And so, while it is our work, it is work that is done in response to the invitation and call of God. Our work is a vocation, meaning that we speak and act in response to the call of the ascended Christ, whose compelling invitation forms and transforms the meaning of our work. For the apostle Paul there was no doubt: his vocation came in direct response to his encounter with the ascended Christ on the road to Damascus. What is also of note is that the apostle was often autobiographical in his epistles, whether in reference back to how he knew his readers personally or when he spoke of the calling of God on his life. The longest and most extensive such reflection is found in the Second Letter to the Corinthians. And this section of Paul's correspondence with this church community is an exquisite window into what it means to do what we are called to do—the work or vocation we have in the world—in the meantime. It provides us, Paul's readers, with a remarkable example of what it means to engage the good work to which we are called and do it in light of the ascension.

The text of 2 Corinthians 2–7 is deeply personal—an extraordinary insight into the inner life of the apostle. One cannot but be taken with his transparent and non-sentimental reflection on the challenges of his work and ministry. Much of what he says is unique and particular to him and his calling. Of course. But there are principles—universals—that emerge here that are applicable to all Christian believers as they think about vocation, work, and career.

This needs to be stressed—we are not all little apostles, variations on the apostle Paul. Further, much of what Paul writes here reflects the specific challenges he was having with the church in Corinth and may not have parallel significance for each of us. The apostle Paul's calling was unique; his apostolic ministry was specific to his time and place; and his engagement with the church in Corinth was of that time. But we can still appreciate how the vision of life, work, and ministry that emerges from his reflections on his vocation has relevance for all of us.

These five chapters—2 Corinthians 2, 3, 4, 5, 6, and the opening verses of chapter 7—reflect a variety of themes and convictions. Noteworthy is that they are not expressed in a clear logical sequence. In his commentary on 2 Corinthians, Ralph P. Martin observes that in this passage that Paul uses a literary device which Martin speaks of as a "ring-composition," meaning that he makes some preliminary observations or affirmations and then at a later point reverts to these earlier statements to "complete the circle of ideas."[9] And so perhaps the most helpful approach to Paul's reflections is to identify key themes—the threads that run throughout these chapters—and suggest how their meaning intersects and how each thread reinforces the other and how each of these themes might have continuing relevance for all of those who are thinking about what it means to do our work, our vocations in the world, in response to the ascended Christ. Here

---

9. Martin, *2 Corinthians*, 75.

we have an enduring testimony to what it means to be engaged, personally, in the mission of God in the world, in a way that is deeply informed by the ascension and in anticipation of the consummation of the kingdom that is yet to come.

The New Covenant

First, Paul intentionally and explicitly locates his calling, his vocation, within the context of the new covenant: "God . . . has made us ministers of the new covenant, not of letter but of spirit, for the letter kills, but the Spirit gives life"(2 Cor 3:6).

He speaks of the older covenant, under the law, which is past tense; and then he speaks of the new covenant established *in Christ*. The apostle is not dismissive of the law; he recognizes that it served a good purpose. But it was parenthetical, in part because it had the effect of being like a "veil" whereby the full glory of God is hidden. It is hidden, of course, pending the revelation of God in Christ Jesus, through whom and by whom the character and redemptive work of God make sense. Thus the Mosaic covenant has been superseded by the coming and ascension of Christ (4:1, 16). And yet, Paul clearly knows that this time—this window in history, what I am speaking of here as "in the meantime"—is a *temporary* season. It is not the final consummation. He is well aware of and lives in light of the day when, as he puts it, this earthly body/tent will pass away (5:1–10). This does not entail that our lives do not have meaning or that we live only for what is yet to come. It is only a matter of perspective: our work matters, but we see it in the big picture of knowing that we can be hopeful in the confidence that good will triumph in the end.

This is the grace we seek: to be fully present to this world, at this time—100 percent present and engaged—while all the while knowing that the full consummation is yet to come. All work is not done under this new order—what we might speak of as an eschatological age: between the first and second coming of Christ, the age of the Spirit. Now in Christ all things are being made new (5:17). Paul responds to this situation—this new age—with a distinct enthusiasm: it is the "day of salvation"—a day not to become a recluse but to be an instrument of reconciliation in the world. We can enthusiastically embrace the work to which we are called, with hope, courage, and alacrity.

In the Meantime

Consider then how all Christians might think of vocation through this same lens: that our work in the church and in the world is found within this dispensation—this new covenant context, the age of the Spirit. Paul and the other apostles and all those called into pastoral office and ministry obviously locate their vocations within the context of the new covenant; but my point is that this surely applies to one and all. Work under the old covenant mattered; it was good work. The difference now is that, in the language of Jesus himself, the kingdom of God has come—not yet in its fullness, for sure, but it has come. Now, all Christians live their lives in worship of the ascended Lord and do their work as participants in the reconciling work of the same ascended Lord. We are not merely waiting for the consummation of the kingdom. We are, even now—regardless of our vocations—witnesses to and participants in the kingdom work of God in the world.

Even now, we read, all things are being reconciled to God in Christ (Col 1:20). We affirm this with an appropriate caution: we are not working to establish Christ's kingdom (the error of Christian nationalism). We do our work fully aware that we are in the in-between and liminal space of the first and second comings of Christ. And so, we do not overstate the presence of the kingdom. But we also do not underestimate what it means to be ministers in and under and in witness to the new covenant in Christ Jesus.

Can we find this "sweet spot"—to be fully present to this age while graciously waiting for the age to come? Can we be in but not of—or, in the language of 1 Peter, can we be gracious *exiles* (1 Pet 1:1–2) who are the living witness to Christ, fully present to this time and place without overstating what can happen in this time and in this place? Can we be all-in to this time and this place while patiently awaiting the full inbreaking of the reign of God at the consummation of the kingdom? The image of the exile is particularly helpful: we are fully here, we are very much resident in this time and place and yet (and yet!) we know that the fullness of the reign of Christ is still to come.

Vocation as Service

If we can find this sweet spot, it will be as we embrace the vision of vocation as an act of *service*. What is very clear in the 2 Corinthians reflections of the apostle is that any sense of vocation he has is rooted in and finds expression in a commitment to generous, radical, and sacrificial service for the risen and ascended Christ.

Vocation and Work in the Meantime

Vocation was not, for the apostle, all about him. And it is not about us. Rather, it is an act of service. It is an act of response to the call of Christ and for Christ and for the life of the world. As Paul puts it, it is not ourselves that we preach, but Christ. It is not about ego, or reputation, or significance. It is not about establishing a legacy. It is about Christ and his reign. This is the very essence of "vocation": service.

A government official is a servant to her constituents—whether as mayor of this city or as a federal minister or representative. If you are a teacher, this is your vision: to serve those who have enrolled in your class. It is their flourishing that matters for you. If you are in business, it is not about you or your brand or your profits. The brand is about a product or service that will meet a human need or cultivate human flourishing. A business can be an act of service from beginning to end: the shoe repair shop that makes sure these shoes meet the needs of the customers; the bookstore that serves authors and readers. If you are in sales—you "park" the huge pressure to meet a sales quota and honestly ask yourself before you close the deal: Is this purchase right for this person? The real estate agent does not press a young buyer to overreach in the purchase of a house. In all cases, we ask, as a matter of course, "How can I be of service?"

Related to this is the integrity question. Paul speaks of "peddlers of God's word" as an indictment of those who are not truly in service mode. Could it be that within every occupation—literally *every* calling—there is this integrity question: whether in business, teaching, politics, or the arts, there are those who bring quality and integrity to the task and to what it means to be of service to a client, customer, student, parishioner, or constituent?

And there are those who are mere peddlers of a service or a product, or for lack of a better word, "hacks." Perhaps they are in this line of work for the sake of their personal need for affirmation or in an attempt to make a quick dollar. As artists, they only produce kitsch; in business, their products have no inherent integrity or beauty or even true function, or they build in obsolescence as a way to foster dependence rather than lasting value. As politicians, they shamelessly lie or fuel the fears of their constituents as a way to get votes. As religious leaders, they tell stories that bring them acclaim rather than speaking with a gracious and simple faithfulness to the ancient text.

Our service is first and foremost an act of response to the ascended Christ. We are in the world as those who have chosen to be in service for Christ. And so it follows that when we speak about vocation, work, and career, we use the language of "for"—that, in some form or another, we are working for Jesus and for his kingdom. We are working for Jesus—we are, in the language of 2 Corinthians, giving ourselves in generous and radical service "for Jesus' sake" (2 Cor 4:11). We let go of the need to be acclaimed and grow in our capacity for living and working in obscurity if and as this is consistent with our calling.

And yet, we can go further. There is a fascinating nuance that emerges in the remarks of the apostle Paul. He certainly views his life as an act of service for Christ. But more, he clearly also views his work in the world as something that he is doing *with* Christ. The apostle speaks of how we are ambassadors—a metaphor that signals that we represent Christ and are working for him in the world, that Christ, as he puts it, makes an appeal *through* the apostle (2 Cor 5:20). But then the apostle shifts ever so quickly to the language of "with" and opens chapter 6 with this perspective in saying "as we work together with him" (2 Cor 6:1).

The whole of this section of the Letter to the Corinthians pivots here: Paul is not merely an observer of the work of the ascended Christ in the world; Paul is a participant, at work with Christ—engaging his talent and his energy and his skill not just for Christ but *with* Christ. And with him we come to see that our work is not our agenda or dream or messianic vision, but rather as mere participant in what God is doing in Christ by the Spirit in this time and in this place.

This means that we are not merely serving Christ—fulfilling marching orders, getting stuff done for Jesus. The relationship with Christ, in our work, is not utilitarian. We are partners: participants in what Jesus is doing; we are co-workers.

Can we speak of our work as something that we are doing *with* Christ— who by the Spirit gives us words to speak such that Christ speaks through us and that in the Spirit we are the hands and feet of Jesus in the world? Can we affirm that we are not mere busybodies frenetically doing the work of God for God, but rather that we are discerners who ask where and how we are to act or not act, speak or not speak, where and as appropriate?

In this we must stress that there is never a one-to-one continuity between the work of Christ and our work. There is never a perfect alignment. And yet, there is profound joy and meaning when we know that in planting this tree, in preaching this sermon, in performing this heart surgery, in teaching this class of fifth graders, in launching this new business—a restaurant, an auto supply shop, a coffee roaster and supplier—that in some mysterious and powerful sense, we are with Christ in the world. We never presume. We all know the arrogance and narcissism of those who think of themselves as little gods, proto-messiahs, who do not question their motives or methods. And yet the times will come when we feel this alignment with the universe—the sense that the Spirit has gifted us and empowered us for a particular task or responsibility.

Our Humility and Our Confidence

Then also, the apostle speaks to the *confidence* we have in the work to which we called. In Paul's autobiographical reflections, there are a string of remarks that address matters of competence, his self-confidence in his ministry, and the question of capacity and even *adequacy* for the work to which he was called. And this has relevance to all—whether athletes or teachers or pastors or business entrepreneurs or artists or civic leaders or nonprofit managers.

And so the apostle raises the question of his competency and qualifications for the job. It would seem that part of the debate that Paul had with those of the church in Corinth was whether he was truly certified for his role and responsibility as an apostle. They dismissed him, it seems, challenging whether he was truly anointed for this work—questioning his credentials. Some doubted the apostle's qualifications because of his suffering. Ralph Martin notes "the 'triumphalist' tenor of [his] opponents . . ."[10] In summary, they discounted Paul because he lacked what they viewed to be the appropriate credentials. And he suffered. Further, they seem to have questioned whether the apostle had ever had a true anointing.

In response, the apostle has no problem accepting his limitations. He knows he is but a vessel of clay—signaling his humanity and confirming his vulnerability. He has no illusions; he is no messiah. He fully accepts "who is capable or equipped for this?" What I find noteworthy is that he does not appeal to ecstatic signs or miracles; he does not speak about a mystical experience that might authenticate his ministry or work for his hearers. He does not even claim a special anointing—something that we all too frequently hear from both government and religious leaders. As Martin puts it, "if he had visionary experiences—on which his opponents prided themselves—they were moments of intimacy between God and himself, and not to be paraded as flamboyant claims."[11]

---

10. Martin, *2 Corinthians*, 47.
11. Martin, *2 Corinthians*, 127.

And yet, while the apostle was put on the defensive and being dismissed, he writes with an uncanny confidence. He knew his calling and vocation and he did what he needed to do. He wrote to the Corinthians as an apostle with the full authority of the office. But he did so all while being discredited as inauthentic and he did so fully aware of his own limitations. Can we find this same sweet spot—not heroism or arrogance or any thought that we are proto-messiahs or that we have a special anointing and are thus God's gift to the church and the world, but also, not a false humility that we are but "worms" with nothing to offer, discounting or even disparaging the quality and character of our work? Can we find a quiet and understated confidence that we are here for this time and in this place and need to do what needs to be done? And can we do it without either overstating our significance or conversely discrediting ourselves and dismissing the value of our work?

During my first pastoral ministry in a small city in Ontario, I found myself in a deeply conflicted congregation that had gone through a church split and still bore the scars of it. Again and again it crossed my mind: this is too much for me; I am in over my head; this congregation needs a far more experienced, wise, and skilled pastor to navigate this complicated and convoluted situation. I felt I had neither the experience nor skill to lead a congregation where conflict seemed to be in the very DNA of their common life.

Toward the end of my first year there, we had a guest speaker come to town—for a series of evening talks and weekend ministry: the Reverend Bob Willoughby. He was brilliant: he spoke with authority and wisdom; he very early on named the problem and challenged those who continued to fuel the conflict; and he spoke with grace and hopefulness about the future. I was in awe. This was precisely what I thought our congregation needed—not just for that weekend but for the next number of months and years.

After the last session, at home that evening over a cup of tea, I said as much to Bob. I told him that he was wise, experienced, and courageous, and this congregation could use someone of his capacity. I will never forget his response: without discounting what he had brought to the ministry he had brought to us, without any false humility or denial of his contribution, he simply said: "Well, Gordon, perhaps; but you are the one called to be their pastor; you have been placed here. And in dependence on God you can do what needs to be done in this place." He fully acknowledged that it was a huge challenge, but his point remained: I was the one called to provide religious leadership for that congregation at that time.

Regardless of our vocations—artist, teacher, business entrepreneur, pastor—there will be skeptics and naysayers who are not impressed by our work. And we will have our own doubts as well; many of us find that our most harsh critic is ourselves. The response is not to insist we are brilliant: the best restauranteur! The best artist ever! Rather, we just do what we have been assigned to do. Without comparisons; without a false humility; but also without overstating how capable we are. We bring talent and ability and diligence without assuming that we are messiahs or super-human or even particularly extraordinary. We have no inclination to be the GOAT (the greatest of all time) or establish a legacy. We just need to be true to our calling at this time and this place. We do not need our name in lights. We do not need to be famous, or need to have a staggering number of "likes" in our social media posts. We do not need to claim a special anointing.

We let all that go; and we choose to be faithful in the exercise of the gifts, talents, and capacities we have been given. We attend to what needs to be done. We say what needs to be said—no more and no less.

Also, we accept when a role or responsibility is too much for us: we are not qualified and we do not have the experience or skill-mix for what it is that needs to be done. This awareness does not diminish us, but simply serves as a reminder that we are likely best called to serve Christ in a different capacity. And we graciously accept where it is that we fit within the ecology of God's purposes within the world and thus our role or place within a community, business, or organization.

The Way of the Cross

One of the enduring contributions of Paul's reflections in 2 Corinthians is how he considers his work in light of the cross and his identification with the crucified Christ who is now his ascended Lord. The apostle speaks to his own challenges and notes that the work to which he was called was not easy. And in this he makes a remarkable observation: he assumes that "death is at work in us," that "our outer nature is wasting away" (2 Cor 12). His whole posture is one where the cross of Christ is neither distant nor past but very present. In his work—now, this side of the ascension—he bears or carries that cross. The cross informs his life and work and ministry. And this raises the question: Can we speak of the intersection of the cross with every vocation? Are all Christians called to bear the cross? Will a cross of some form intersect the life and work of all?

In the Meantime

Noteworthy here, then, is that the cross is not merely a past tense reference ("Christ died for me"). It is that, of course, but with the apostle it is clear that the whole of life and work is one of living in and bearing the cross. Elsewhere he speaks of how we are "joint heirs with Christ in this suffering" (Rom 8:17). The cross marks us, for each of us our vocations are fulfilled as those who live and work on the "via dolorosa." We not only look back to the cross, we live and work now under the sign of the cross.

As a matter of course, it is helpful to remember that you will be wronged; you will be lied about, misunderstood, underappreciated, misrepresented. Just assume that this is part of the package—almost in the sense that it is precisely because we are faithful in our work that we will create this kind of response. We do not excuse this behavior, but we let it be and choose to respond with generosity.

We do not think of ourselves as martyrs, knowing full well the limitations that we bring to the role or responsibility. We have to be willing to accept genuine criticism of our work. And we may well have someone tell us that we are not suited for or do not have the experience and skill-mix for a role. That is fine and that may well be their prerogative. Further, any kind of martyr complex is antithetical to the quality and character of our vocations and in the end nothing but a form of narcissism. We must be both competent and accountable, both generous and discerning. And a lack of discernment or competency does not invalidate any critique we might receive. Rather, the point is that the road will be a challenging one.

For the apostle Paul, he had quite the list. He opens with being "afflicted in every way." He speaks of being perplexed, persecuted, struck down (2 Cor 4:8–9) and then also of beatings, imprisonments, riots, sleepless nights, hunger, and more (2 Cor 6:4–5). However, he speaks of all of this as "light and momentary troubles" (Cor 4:17, NIV), which may seem a form of pseudo-optimism and denial except that the apostle sees and feels and experiences all of this as part of the groaning of creation and his deep confidence that this is only for now, for a season (Rom 8:18–20). This too will pass (as our mothers told us). Most of all, this grief and pain cannot compare with what is yet to come (2 Cor 5:1). In all of this, I am struck by a line in the journal of Thomas Merton: "I have a peculiar horror of one sin: the exaggeration of our trials and of our crosses."[12]

Therefore, the apostle insists, we do not lose heart (2 Cor 4:16). Or putting it differently, we do not give in to despair (4:8). Rather, we are

---

12. Merton, *Sign of Jonas*, 6.

Vocation and Work in the Meantime

marked by a resilient hopefulness. To this end, Paul calls his readers to the purposeful cultivation of the interior life. Even though there is wear and tear on his physical well-being—the challenges of his vocation—he insists that his "inmost self" was experiencing renewal, as he and his peers set their eyes on what is unseen (not what is seen) (4:18).

Tending to one's interior well-being is pivotal: we cannot allow the challenges and griefs along the way to settle into our hearts and, in the language of another text, "harden" our hearts (Heb 3:15). We cannot allow bitterness to take root on our innermost lives (Heb 12:15). The more grief we experience, the greater this imperative that we find time and space for the spiritual practice of sabbath disengagement, mutual encouragement with friends, the walk in the woods or on the beach, praying the Psalms, and engaging with the arts.

We refuse to allow resentment and accumulated grievances take root within us, robbing us of joy, weighing down our spirits. We feel the full force of the fragmented universe and we know this grief when it touches our personal lives, when it impacts our relationships, our work, our physical and economic well-being and that of those that we love. But, and this is the key, we get angry, but anger is not our emotional default; we know fear, but we cast our cares on he who cares for us (1 Peter 5); we get discouraged, but we do not allow our hearts to be filled with cynicism and despair.

Bottom line, we sustain a resilient hopefulness even in the midst of the pain and loss. We suffer but, as the apostle stresses, we do not suffer as those who have no hope (Rom 8:18–20), but as those who know that ultimately all will be healed and made well. We are not oblivious to the pain of this world. We are not living happy-clappy lives of disengagement from the sorrows of this world. We know and feel the pain of this world. But we are not consumed by this sorrow for the very simple reason that we know it is only for a season. Most of all we do not view suffering as an aberration, but rather as a means by which we identify with Christ. We are drawn into fellowship with him, united with him, joint heirs with him, in his suffering (Rom 8:17).

Knowing the Love of Christ

Finally, with the apostle Paul, we come to the bottom line. We come full circle and affirm that "the love of Christ compels us" (2 Cor 5:14). This is the heart and soul of our personal and solitary encounter with God in prayer: to know Christ and the love of Christ, which then the apostle insists is precisely that which is the guiding energy of our lives and our work. The love of God in Christ that "urges us on." The love of God sustains us through weal and woe. The love of God provides us with the orientation and sustaining grace for the facing of our circumstances. And as stressed already, it is a personal knowledge of the love of God in Christ, granted to us and communicated to us through our solitary encounter with Christ in our prayers.

That is, we begin and end from this posture and disposition: our love for Christ is in response to Christ's love for us; and our generous service for others, as an act of Christian love, is but because we were first loved by Christ. It is this love that empowers us to serve others with generosity, not concerned with our legacy or reputation or our "name." As Ralph Martin puts it, "Christ's love . . . was the dominating force of the Apostles' life."[13] And so it is no surprise to read the benediction and prayer that we find in the Ephesian correspondence:

> . . . that Christ may dwell in your hearts through faith, as you are being rooted and grounded in love. I pray that you may have the power to comprehend, with all the saints, what is the breadth and length and height and depth and to know the love of Christ that surpasses knowledge, so that you may be filled with all the fullness of God. (Eph 3:17–19)

We know the grace of a benevolent God as we join with God's people in worship each week; and in our personal prayers, this is the God we know, the God who has been revealed to us in Christ, who is the living embodiment of the love of God.

The Importance of Spiritual Practice

Can we do this? With the apostle, can we find this sweet spot, knowing what it means to be fully present to Christ and to do the work of Christ to which Christ calls us, but hold it lightly? Can we be fully engaged without thinking either that we are heroes or descending into a false self-deprecation? Can we live and work compelled by the love of God?

Yes, we can. But surely we need to be intentional. Of necessity we need to speak of critical and essential spiritual practices—viewing a "practice"

---

13. Martin, *2 Corinthians*, 129.

as a tangible means and a habituated routine by which we appropriate the grace of God for that which lies before and around us. Or, more specifically, we view spiritual practice as the means by which the Spirit cultivates and nurtures our capacity to be found in Christ. Spiritual practice becomes then a means of grace—an exercise by which we lift up our hearts and set our minds on Christ, the ascended high priest and cosmic Lord, even as the Spirit does what only the Spirit can do in the transformation of our inner selves. By way of example, consider three spiritual practices in particular: the spiritual journal, spiritual conversation, and praying the Psalms.

The Spiritual Journal

Second Corinthians 2–7 is an example of the apostle reflecting on the movements of his own heart. It is a form of spiritual autobiography, or perhaps we could speak of it as his journal—a spiritual journal—that he includes in his letter to the Corinthian church. Here we find the apostle reflecting on the movements of his own interior life and experience and writing about it.

There is a long tradition or history of this kind of written reflection in the Western Christian heritage—with noteworthy contributions from Augustine of Hippo, Ignatius of Loyola, John Wesley, Leo Tolstoy, Thomas Merton, Dorothy Day, and many others. It has a long pedigree and there may be something to the line attributed to Tolstoy, that he discerned his vocation in the pages of his journal.

In speaking of spiritual practices that inform the work to which we are called—spiritual disciplines that inform and sustain our sense of vocational awareness and engagement—might the spiritual journal be an invaluable spiritual practice?

This is different from a diary, where one might simply record the activities of the day. Rather, is a reflection piece, though perhaps with regular entries that reference the events in our lives: perhaps not daily but at the very least weekly, where we think about and make sense of what is happening to us vocationally. A spiritual journal is personal and private reflection on how our engagement with the world, notably through our vocations, has informed or left traces in our interior lives. With a spiritual journal, we tend or are aware of to the movements of our hearts: what is happening, and more specifically, what are we feeling in response to what is happening? The journal becomes a means for becoming more emotionally self-aware.

We cannot stress this next point too strongly: the journal only serves its purpose if we are honest. This is a private space; this is not a memoir that we will publish. Instead, this is a space where before God we speak to the reality of what we are experiencing. With transparent and growing self-awareness we speak of what it means to be in the world as those who know the ascended Christ—and specifically the love of the ascended Christ—in real time. A spiritual journal frees us to name the reality of our experience and our interior response to that experience. We move behind denial and living a lie; we become more and more self-aware. And most of all, we see the grace and benevolence of God in our own lives and in our own experience: the journal is the reminder that we can sing "Great is thy Faithfulness . . . Lord, unto me."

The Gift of Spiritual Conversation

Life in communion with the ascended Lord and ministry and work and engagement in the world "with Christ" assumes or presumes the capacity for solitude—as noted in chapter 4. But solitude needs an essential complement: the company of others. We cannot do that to which we are called if we are alone. We can only navigate the complexities—notably the *emotional* complexities of life and work—if we have companions on the road: peers and elders with whom our interior lives are brought to the surface as an exercise in "sense making" but also accountability.

We meet with someone a generation older than ourselves to consider what we are experiencing—someone who is an elder-friend-mentor or spiritual director. And we meet with one or two peers—friends on the way, companions at the coffee shop, or on the extended and leisured walk on the weekend. We reflect together on joys and sorrows and grow in our capacity for both emotional self-awareness and resilience. And, perhaps most of all, we encourage one another. This becomes a vital complement to shared worship as another means by which we are in communion with the ascended Christ as those who are in community. Spiritual friendship is a concrete and tangible expression of this. Our personal fellowship with the ascended Christ presumes that we are in community and that we are cultivating the companionship of friends and elders along the way, where together we remind one another that God is good—all the time.

The Psalms

Three spiritual practices. The spiritual journal. Spiritual friendship. And then third, reading and praying the Psalms. This practice merits a whole chapter. To this, then, we turn.

7

Praying the Psalms

IF WE TAKE THE ascension seriously, we will pray the Psalms. If we attend to the call of Colossians 3:2—and set our hearts and minds above, where Christ is seated at the right hand of the Father—we will pray the Psalms. If in the midst of the challenges of life and work and ministry we are keen to look to Jesus, the author of our faith, and to know the love of God in Christ Jesus in our hearts, we will pray the Psalms.

With the Psalms we are praying with Christ, our high priest. But more, the Psalms bring head and heart, longing and desire into alignment with Christ. The Psalms are the means—what Eugene Petersen speaks of as "tools"[1]—by which we live now, in the meantime, in light of the ascension. On the one hand we are praying with Christ; but then further, in praying the Psalms—as habituated practice—our minds and hearts are increasingly *aligned* with the heart and mind of the ascended Christ. We see and feel the world, and our place in the world, in light of the ascension.

In praying the Psalms, we are in continuity with the historic witness of the church—from Origen to Athanasius to Augustine, and then through the entire Benedictine monastic tradition where the Psalms were the content of the daily office and the prayers that anchored and gave structure to their common life. More recently, we have the witness of Dietrich Bonhoeffer, C. S. Lewis, Eugene Peterson, and N. T. Wright—all of

---

1. Peterson, *Answering God*.

whom would say some variation of what Wright observes: that the Psalms are indispensable to Christian corporate worship and to the personal prayers of the individual Christian.[2]

Thus the neglect of the Psalms in much contemporary Christian worship is reason for concern if not alarm. We do not need to go as far as the older Scottish Presbyterians who as of midway through the seventeenth century would sing only the Psalms. And yet, we have perhaps swung too far the other way, such that for many Christians the Psalms only play an incidental role in Christian worship—perhaps a line or two here and there.

In an age of distraction, when it is challenging to keep our hearts and minds focused and present to Christ, we pray the Psalms. Not in one reading; but as habituated practice: we do it again and again and again. The Psalms in our daily prayers and in the weekly worship of the faith community, day in and day out, and over time, bring our hearts and minds into alignment with Christ. When we find that our hearts are leaning towards anger, fear, or discouragement, it is through the Psalms that we come to consolation, the interior disposition of those who in the meantime live and work, in light of the ascension.

We pray the Psalms as regular and routine practice. And gradually but surely nothing matters more but the joy of coming to know, love, and desire to serve Jesus, the ascended Christ. If, as a pastor, you want a congregation that longs to know Jesus, love Jesus, and serve Jesus, maturing as disciples of Christ, then lead them in worship with the Psalms.

If as a congregation you want to learn what it means to live in light of the kingdom and to respond to the call of Jesus to seek first the kingdom of God, you will assure that the Psalms are central to shared worship and you will encourage one and all to pray the Psalms as part of their personal spiritual practice. In the language of the sixteenth- and seventeenth-century spiritual writers, what is cultivated and nurtured within us is a "holy indifference"—a capacity to desire nothing but the will of God.

And it is important to stress that what the Psalms do, collectively, is foster within us a deepening *trust* in the ascended Christ. If we are saved by faith then it follows that we grow and mature in the faith and we journey on the road of life and we come to greater healing and wholeness even as and specifically as we learn to trust. The Psalms fuel this capacity for faith in the living and ascended Lord precisely because of the rich theological content

---

2. See Wright, *Case for the Psalms*—notably the case he makes in the introduction to this small volume.

of the Psalms, but then also because they are the means by which head and heart are integrated.

I need to add the following: There are those who insist that we should not personalize the Psalms. They insist that the Psalms are not about us but rather that these are the prayers of David and then the prayers of Christ. And yet, consider the counter-argument: when we pray the psalms of David and as such identify with him, we see his experience through the lens of our own journey of faith. We enter into the dynamic of how Christ himself is our high priest and Lord and that we are praying *with* him. And so our praying is not in the abstract, but very much as those who are in this world and feeling the full force of both the goodness and fragmentation of this world. And so, as we read and pray the Psalms more and more, they become intensely personal and inevitably autobiographical. Thus William Brown notes that in praying the Psalms our joys and sorrows are viewed through the experience of Christ. They become a means by which we are aligned, heart, soul, and mind, with Christ Jesus. So yes, we can and must contend that these then become our prayers, but if and only as they are first the prayers of the ascended Christ Jesus—our high priest and king.

Study the Psalms. As a precursor to your prayers and as you pray the Psalms, study them to appreciate both their theological content as well as the affect that is being expressed. In the classic essay from the early church *On the Incarnation*, Athanasius concludes with an appendix, a letter from Athanasius to Marcellinus on the Psalms. And he notes that Marcellinus is ill and on his sickbed and, as Athanasius puts it, he has chosen "using the leisure necessitated by your recent illness to study" the whole of the Scriptures "and especially the Psalms."[3] As he concludes his reflections he urges Marcellinus to ponder the Psalms and read them intelligently, with the Spirit as his guide.[4] That is classic counsel: ponder the Psalms, read them intelligently, lean into the Spirit as your guide as you pray them.

When we study the Psalms, several things come to our attention. We learn to attend to Hebrew parallelism, for example, and see how just two lines in a Psalm, read and sung together, draw us into fellowship with Christ. The first line sets us up; the second draws us in. Consider, for example, Psalm 17. The prayer of verse 6 begins with "I call upon you, for you will answer me, O God," and the follow-up parallel prayer draws us in:

---

3. Athanasius, *On the Incarnation*, 97.
4. Athanasius, *On the Incarnation*, 119.

Praying the Psalms

"Incline your ear to me, hear my words," reflecting our deep longing that God would attend to the cry of our hearts.

But most importantly, as we get to know the Psalms, we recognize that the Psalms are of a whole and that some psalms are more pivotal in shaping the overall way in which the Psalms are presented and received. The order or sequence of the Psalms is not arbitrary. There is a deep logic to what we find here—to the sequence of the Psalms from Psalm 1 through Psalm 150.

William Brown observes that Psalms 1 and 2 are like the two lenses of a pair of glasses: that what is said and prayed and sung in these two psalms are the two defining threads that run throughout the Psalter.[5] They provide what N. T. Wright speaks of as a "worldview"—the essential perspective for all life, like a pair of spectacles through which we view our lives and our world.[6] We remember that as a rule each psalm celebrates God as creator or redeemer—or, in so many cases, as both. This is foundational to our lives and to our prayers. The one whom we worship and serve is the creator of all things—and thus we celebrate the beauty and glory of creation (see Psalm 104) and the creator in turns looks with compassion on all he has made and seeks its redemption. And in praying the Psalms we not only delight in the creation but live in the deep confidence that one day all will be restored and healed.

Of particular note is that the Psalms as a whole lead us from lament to joy-filled thanksgiving. The Psalms bring us into the presence of the ascended Christ not as an escape from the world: they are not sentimental. Rather, the Psalms give us the words to say and pray and sing by which we bring the felt awareness of our fragmented world and our experience of that world into the company of Christ. We are in worship, through the Psalms, as those who are very much in the world: and thus we lean into the psalms of lament as well as the psalms of thanksgiving and blessing. We pray as those who identify with the whole redemptive work of God—the God whom the Psalms celebrate as the creator and redeemer of all things.

And so we are drawn into communion with God—specifically into the law of God, the wisdom of God, without which we cannot live with sanity and grace in the world. The Psalms mediate to us the grace of living in the world as those who are "in but not of"—living in light of the ascension but knowing that the full expression of the kingdom is yet to come. There is no triumphalism; there is no hopelessness: both pseudo-positivity and

---

5. Brown, *Psalms*, 113.
6. Wright, *Case for the Psalms*, 7.

hopeless despair are confronted by the Psalms. We find the true grace of what it means to live "in the meantime." When our desires and longings are misguided and out of alignment with the good, the noble, and the excellent, ancient sources remind us that the Psalms are the central way by which we know the ordering of our affections and bring heart and mind into alignment with the ascended Christ.

When we come to Psalm 110 we come to the mountaintop in its witness to the king who is now high priest and ruler over all. We have a whole theology of the ascension in this one psalm.

> The Lord says to my lord,
> "Sit at my right hand
> until I make your enemies your footstool."
> like dew, your youth will come to you.
>
> The Lord has sworn and will not change his mind,
> "You are a priest forever according to the order of Melchizedek."
> (Psalm 110:1 and 4)

And we come to Psalm 147. This psalm celebrates the gracious work of God, and reflects the deep confidence of the people of God that God is on the throne of the universe, that God is good and powerful and wise. We lean into the God of all goodness, power, and wisdom; and in knowing this, we give thanks and make melody and extol the Lord.

And yet, we also know that all is not well. Psalm 147 speaks of how God gives food to the animals, but we know that there are God's creatures that are going extinct. And the psalm affirms that God cares for the downtrodden (verse 6), but we all know of those whose homes are being destroyed even as they struggle with the basics of life—as they live in a war zone or in drought or through a climate crisis or through the usual challenges of family and work, and perhaps even significant division in the life of the church. They feel downtrodden or they ache for those who are in crisis; we know and feel the fragmentation of this world. So, can we pray Psalm 147 knowing what we know? How can those who live and work in deeply compromised situations—even war zones—pray and sing this psalm?

Quite simply, because Psalm 147 is not a stand-alone text, but rather an integral part of the whole of the witness of the Psalms that unequivocally recognizes the deep fragmentation and pain of our world. Psalm 23 speaks of the dark valley, Psalm 46 of a time of trouble. The Psalms demonstrate a remarkable transparency and honesty about the human condition. We read

Praying the Psalms

and sing to see Psalm 147 in this context. And yet, what we can say is that when all is said and done, when you come to the end of the Psalms, you turn a corner: and again and again the goodness, power, and wisdom of God is extolled. And we are called to hope (Ps 147:11) in the steadfast love of God. This becomes our default orientation, and it means that our default disposition of heart is one of consolation.

What is fascinating is that the psalms of lament are concentrated towards the earlier parts of the book. And while threads of lament continue all the way through till Psalm 102 and Psalm 109, by the time we come to Psalm 147 we have not just turned the corner, we have arrived. For myself, the inflection point is Psalm 95. I see and feel that despite all that we know is wrong in our world, we give thanks for the goodness, wisdom, and benevolent power of God. With honesty—no illusion, no sentimentality, no pseudo-optimism or denial of the wrong, but very specifically in the context of our lament—we give thanks and give praise and adoration to Christ who is our high priest and cosmic Lord. And in this we rest; in this we find our consolation.

All of this suggests that the Psalms should play a vital part in our personal and solitary prayers. Perhaps we learn to pray through the entire Psalter twice a year, praying a psalm a day (with lengthy Psalm 119 prayed over five days). Or, alternatively, we pray through a segment or section of the Psalms each Lent. The important thing is that over time we come to know the Psalter. And then in times of joy and sorrow, or confusion and uncertainly, we know the Psalms and can turn to a psalm that is familiar to us and that gives us the words that need to be said, the prayer that reflects the longing of our heart. All of this, of course, draws us into the presence and company of the ascended Christ. We learn to pray *with* Christ and then also, through the Psalms, we learn what it means to fulfill our vocations with a significant measure of both theological integrity and a resilient hopefulness.

And they are the vital and essential way by which we live in the great promises of the ascension—not only that Christ will return, but that he will be with us to the end. And thus we pray and sing:

> If I take the wings of the morning
> and settle at the farthest limits of the sea,
> even there your hand shall lead me,
> and your right hand shall hold me fast. (Ps 139:9–10)

In the Meantime

The Ordinary and the Numinous

Consider two perspectives that are cultivated in our interior lives when we pray the Psalms.

First, we learn to embrace the ordinary. We come to see that even the most ordinary aspects of our lives have meaning, even the seemingly most mundane activities of our lives. Everything we do has meaning: walking with our children to the school bus stop, teaching a daughter to ride a bicycle, going for coffee with a friend, putting out the bins for recycling—the daily life around the home: it all matters. This is not to discount the more seemingly significant things we do—whether preaching a sermon or conducting a choir or opening a new business or completing a graduate degree. It is merely to stress that by virtue of the ascension our daily and routine experience has meaning and value. We can delight in the ordinary.

Rather than bemoaning what seems like a mundane daily experience, we will live in the moment, present to whatever is part of the day. Rather than craving excitement or assuming that the novel or the extraordinary is what gives life meaning, we will learn to be fully present to the immediate daily experience and rhythms of life. We no longer assume that what gives us joy is the exotic holiday or some fantasy escape from the drudgery of our existence; we have eyes and ears that are present to the immediate.

And it is not only church activities or spiritual practices that give our lives meaning and significance; or that somehow it is only when we are in prayer or at the church or doing religious work that what we are doing matters. All the ordinary matters. The ordinary is sacred time and space. I am not discounting religious practice; of course not. Indeed, we could easily conclude that we cannot appreciate the numinous all around us unless we are women and men of worship and prayer, particularly as we pray and sing the Psalms.

But then of course, it follows: in the midst of the ordinary we are attentive to those moments and events in our lives that call us into an awareness and experience of the numinous. Some are obvious: we get the call and our daughter has given birth and we have the remarkable opportunity to hold a newborn infant in our arms. We stand in the side chapel of the San Luigi dei Francesi Church in Rome and take in the wonder of Caravaggio's *Calling of St. Matthew*. We sit on a park bench and listen to the story of a young man from an utterly secular upbringing describing his growing awareness of the love of God in Christ and his decision to be baptized at a local church. In our daily lives, we can and must be attentive to all the ways in which heaven breaks into our common lives—that is, we are called to sustain an awareness that there is more to reality than merely that which we can taste, touch, feel, and see.

We do not need a cruise in the Caribbean or a trip to Disney World or a resort escape; rather, each day gives witness to the transcendent. It may be watching a pair of barn swallows teach their fledglings to fly. Or enjoying seeing a dog at full tilt chase down a ball in the local school yard. Or the magic of dappled sunlight as we make our way on a path through a woodland. Or the still waters of a lake or the vista from higher up on a green valley below.

An extraordinary example of this can be found in the memoir of Nien Cheng, who lived through a period of solitary confinement during the Cultural Revolution in China. She speaks of how one afternoon she noticed a spider climbing up one of the rusted bars of the window of her cell and she watched as it spun its web—which for Cheng was "intricately beautiful and absolutely perfect." And she noted, she had witnessed something "beautiful and uplifting," for which she thanked God. It reminded her that "God was in control," not Mao Tse-Tung and his revolutionaries, and her "depressing feeling of complete isolation was broken . . ."[7]

The natural order can provide us with a reminder of the numinous but then, of course, we can also turn to the arts: whether the string quartets of Mozart or that moment in Handel's *Messiah* when the soprano eases into "I know that my Redeemer liveth . . ." Or, still in the *Messiah*, the trumpet solo in "The Trumpet Shall Sound." And we revel in the work of less prominent artists and musicians whose work we have come to know and treasure. We keep a tenderheartedness such that our inner sensibilities are not merely engaged in the rational or logical, but also with mystery.

We have eyes and ears attentive to the numinous—those moments that transcend the rational and touch our most inner self; we sustain a sense of mystery. We can and must be intentional and never take anything in our day for granted, but rather stop to see the rainbow, note the beauty of the young boy on his bicycle, recall a line from a favorite poet that happens to come to mind. While the first and most fundamental meaning of transcendence is the person of Christ himself—the ascended Christ—the whole of creation can and does witness to beauty and to the glory of God. If we let it. And if we let the Psalms cultivate this within us—an appreciation of the ordinary and a recognition of the numinous.

7. Cheng, *Life and Death in Shanghai*, 180–81.

In the Meantime

Again, to stress: It is in learning to pray the Psalms that we grow in our capacity to live with this resilient hopefulness. Back to Nien Cheng, and her experience in solitary confinement. She writes:

> In the drab surroundings of the grey cell, I had experienced magic moments of transcendency that I had not experienced in the ease and comfort of my normal life. . . . My belief in the ultimate triumph of truth and goodness had been restored and I had renewed courage to fight on.[8]

What the Psalms give us is something that grows within us: we come to see that joy is our default mode—the natural way of our hearts. Over time we do not grow old and bitter, disappointed with life and with people. Rather, the older we get the sweeter we become; joy resides in our bones and we delight each day in the wonder of God's creation and the reminders of the love of God in Christ, routinely again and again praying and singing the words of Psalm 100.

We are women and men who know that we are called to live and work in the meantime, in light of the ascension. And it is the ascension and our awareness of alignment with the ascended Christ that makes all the difference in the world.

The Way of Consolation

So, when all is said and done, what is the evidence that we are living in the meantime—in light of the ascension? What is the evidence—using the language of Colossians 3:1–2—that we have set our minds on things above? If the ascension is our intellectual, moral point of reference, what is the defining indicator that this is our reality? If our participation is in the mission of God in the world, especially in how we personally do the work to which we are called as this very participation, how will we know that this is truly the case?

Perhaps the foundational evidence is not so much how much we get done or how busy we are, or how successful we are, but rather that what defines us is a particular interior disposition. Or, stating it differently, the posture of our hearts. Might it be that nothing so defines us, to use the language of the sixteenth- and seventeenth-century spiritual guides, as the way of *consolation*.

---

8. Cheng, *Life and Death in Shanghai*, 427.

Praying the Psalms

Jesus makes two remarkable promises to his disciples as he anticipates his ascension—the first recorded for us in John 14 and the second in John 15. In John 14 Jesus anticipates ascension and speaks of the peace that he will give to his disciples—even as he speaks of the coming of the Spirit.

> I have said these things to you while I am still with you. But the Advocate, the Holy Spirit, whom the Father will send in my name, will teach you everything and remind you of all that I have said to you. Peace I leave with you; my peace I give to you. I do not give to you as the world gives. Do not let your hearts be troubled, and do not let them be afraid. (John 14:26-27)

This is matched or echoed in the call of the apostle Paul:

> Do not be anxious about anything, but in everything by prayer and supplication with thanksgiving let your requests be made known to God. And the peace of God, which surpasses all understanding, will guard your hearts and your minds in Christ Jesus. (Phil 4:6-7)

And then, we turn to John 15, where Jesus specifically speaks of joy with the assurance that our joy would be made complete. This comes up again in the prayer that is offered to the Father—recorded for us in John 17—where Jesus prays that his joy would be made complete in the disciples. And then one cannot but be impressed with the language of the apostle Paul, who surely felt the full force of how the kingdom of God had not yet come in fulness as he lived through the trials and tribulations he references in the 2 Corinthians. He outlines all these difficulties and then simply says: "I am overjoyed in all our affliction" (2 Cor 7:4). Or as we read it in another translation: "in all our troubles, our joy knows no bounds . . ." (NIV).

Thus, we speak of a transcendent peace and we speak of complete joy. Could it be that perhaps it is the intersection of peace and joy that is the defining mark of what it means to live in light of the ascension? And if there is a notion or understanding or word that captures this confluence between joy and peace it is surely *consolation*.

Consolation is not—as the word is it is often used—a kind of award or medal for second or third place in the race. As such, consolation is a false comfort—a less-than-ideal outcome. Not what you had hoped for.

But not as it is being used here. Consolation here is the highest expression of the human heart. It is the ultimate sense of well-being. It is the interior assurance that all is well and will be well and that one can rest in the deep confidence of the goodness and purposes of God. It is consolation as the alternative to desolation; it is not an act of denial of the fragmentation of the world; it is not that we do not get angry, sad, discouraged, and afraid. It is instead that desolation does not mark us; it does not define us. Rather, in the magisterial words of the prophet, "you shall go out in joy, and be led back in peace..." (Isa 55:12).

Consolation is contentment—no longer striving or frustrated or worried. We are at peace with ourselves and our world. We rest in the confidence that good will triumph in the end.

Consolation is a resilient joy, even in the midst of a fragmented world. While we may know anger and discouragement, these do not ultimately define us. We are not bitter or resentful or cynical.

Consolation is the profound comfort that is ours when we know we have arrived—we are home. We are no longer striving but letting God be God and letting God do God's work in God's time.

Consolation as the blessings that we associate with the Beatitudes—the consolation of the poor in spirit, those who mourn, those who are meek and hunger for righteousness, the pure in heart, the peacemakers, and those persecuted.

Consolation is the mark of the elders in our midst: the older we are the more at peace we are with God, with ourselves, with others, and with our world.

Perhaps most of all, consolation is the abiding confidence that one is loved—that, more to the point, the creator of the universe looks upon you with a benevolent posture: we know the love of God in Christ, a love that is poured into your heart by the Holy Spirit (Rom 5:5). We are no longer striving for vindication or trying to prove ourselves or wishing that we were loved; we know it and live in this confidence. We abide here.

Thus consolation—a peace that is infused with joy—is surely the mark of those who have learned what it means to live and worship and work in the meantime, in light of the ascension of Christ Jesus. And so we sing.

> Jesus, Thou Joy of loving Hearts
> Thou Fount of life, Thou Light of all;
> From the best bliss that earth imparts
> We turn unfilled to Thee again.

Bibliography

Athanasius. *St. Athanasius on the Incarnation: The Treatise 'de Incarnatione Verbi Dei.'* Translated by a monk of C.S.M.V. London: Mowbray, 1953.
Augustine. Sermon 261. https://www.wesleyscholar.com/wp-content/uploads/2019/04/Augustine-Sermons-273-305.pdf.
Bediako, Kwame. *Jesus in Africa: The Christian Gospel in African History and Experience.* Yaoundé, Cameroon: Editions Cle and Regnum Africa, 2000.
Bloesch, Donald. *Spirituality Old and New: Recovering Authentic Spiritual Life.* Downers Grove, IL: InterVarsity Academic, 2007.
Brown, William P. *Psalms.* Nashville: Abingdon, 2010.
Buchanan, Mark. "Preaching Now and Then." *Faith Today*, July 11, 2022. https://www.faithtoday.ca/Magazines/2022-Jul-Aug-Preaching-Now-And-Then.
Calvin, John. *Institutes of the Christian Religion.* Edited and translated by Henry Beveridge. Grand Rapids: Eerdmans, 1979.
Cheng, Nien. *Life and Death in Shanghai.* London: Grafton, 1986.
Ellul, Jacques. *Apocalypse: The Book of Revelation.* Translated by George W. Schreiner. New York: Seabury, 1977.
———. *False Presence of the Kingdom.* Translated by C. Edward Hopkin. New York: Seabury, 1963.
Farrow, Douglas. *Ascension and Ecclesia: On the Significance of the Doctrine of the Ascension for Ecclesiology and Christian Cosmology.* Grand Rapids: Eerdmans, 1999.
Ignatius. *The Spiritual Exercises of St. Ignatius.* Translated and edited by Louis J. Puhl. N.p.: St. Paul, 1975.
John of the Cross. *The Ascent of Mount Carmel.* In *The Collected Works of St. John of the Cross.* Translated by Kieran Kavanaugh and Otilio Rodriguez. Washington, DC: Institute of Carmelite Studies, 1979.
———. *Living Flame of Love.* In *The Collected Works of St. John of the Cross.* Translated by Kieran Kavanaugh and Otilio Rodriguez. Washington, DC: Institute of Carmelite Studies, 1979.
Julian of Norwich. *Revelations of Divine Love.* Edited by Grace Warrack. London: Methuen, 1911.
———. *Showings.* Translated by Edmund College and James Walsh. New York: Paulist, 1978.

Bibliography

Keener, Craig S. *Acts: An Exegetical Commentary*. Vol 1. Grand Rapids: Baker Academic, 2012.

Lin, Swee Hong, and Lester Ruth. *Lovin' on Jesus: A Concise History of Contemporary Worship*. Nashville: Abingdon, 2017.

Lovelace, Richard F. *Dynamics of Spiritual Life: An Evangelical Theology of Renewal*. Downers Grove, IL: InterVarsity, 1979.

Martin, Ralph P. *2 Corinthians*. Word Biblical Commentary 40. Waco, TX: Word, 1986.

McAlpine, William R. *Sacred Space for the Missional Church: Engaging Culture Through the Built Environment*. Eugene, OR: Wipf and Stock, 2011.

Meacham, Jon. *And There Was Light: Abraham Lincoln and the American Struggle*. New York: Random House, 2022.

Merton, Thomas. *The Sign of Jonas*. New York: Harcourt, Brace and Company, 1953.

Newbigin, Lesslie. *Sign of the Kingdom*. Grand Rapids: Eerdmans, 1980.

Otto, Rudolf. *The Idea of the Holy: An Inquiry into the Non-Rational Factor in the Idea of the Divine and Its Relation to the Rational*. Translated by John W. Harvey. Oxford: Oxford University Press, 1923.

Peterson, Eugene H. *Answering God: The Psalms as Tools for Prayer*. San Francisco: HarperSanFrancisco, 1989.

Pieper, Joseph. *Only the Lover Sings: Art and Contemplation*. Translated by Lothar Krauth. San Francisco: Ignatius, 1990.

Reynolds, Simon. *Lighten Our Darkness: Discovering and Celebrating Choral Evensong*. Croydon, UK: Darton, Longman and Todd, 2021.

Scruton, Roger. *The Face of God: The Gifford Lectures 2010*. New York: Continuum, 2012.

———. *Music as an Art*. London: Bloomsbury Continuum, 2018.

Taylor, Charles. *A Catholic Modernity: Charles Taylor's Marianist Award Lecture*. Edited by James L. Heft. Oxford: Oxford University Press, 1999.

Teresa of Avila. *The Interior Castle*. In *The Collected Works of St. Teresa of Avila*, translated by Kieran Kavanaugh and Otilio Rodriguez. Washington, DC: Institute of Carmelite Studies, 1980.

Tozer, A. W. *The Pursuit of God*. Harrisburg, PA: Christian, 1948.

Webber, Robert. *Ancient-Future Faith: Rethinking Evangelicalism for a Postmodern World*. Grand Rapids: Baker, 1999.

———. *Ancient-Future Worship: Proclaiming and Enacting God's Narrative*. Grand Rapids: Baker, 2008.

Williams, Rowan. *A Silent Action: Engagements with Thomas Merton*. Louisville: Fons Vitae, 2011.

———. *The Wound of Knowledge: Christian Spirituality from the New Testament to St. John of the Cross*. Lanham, MD: Cowley, 1979.

Wright, N. T. *The Case for the Psalms: Why They are Essential*. New York: HarperOne, 2013.

Scripture Index

1 Kings
19:11–12 — 62

2 Kings
2 — 2

Habakkuk
2:20 — 38

Psalms
17 — 102–3
46 — 8, 46
100 — 34
110 — 7–8, 104
139 — 105
147 — 104

Proverbs
4:23 — 13

Isaiah
55:12 — 110

Matthew
5:8 — 11–12
6:33 — 27
28:17 — 1
28:18 — 6

Mark
1:15 — ix
1:14–15 — 1

Luke
24:4–7 — 2
24:32—35 — 34, 41, 42
24:39 — 2

John
6 — 19
10 — 11, 42
10:41 — 2
14 — 1, 4, 9
14:26–27 — 109
14:27 — 14
15:4 — 8
16 — 23

Acts
1:3 — 1
1:4 — 9
1:6 — 2
2:22–36 — 23
2:36 — 6
2:42 — 34
10:41 — 2
13:1–4 — 30, 82

Scripture Index

Romans

5:8	67
8:17	20, 94, 95
8:18–20	95
15:7	84

1 Corinthians

3:6–8	77
13:12	25

2 Corinthians

2—7	86
3:6	87
3:18	49
4:1	87
4:5	43
4:8–9	94
4:11	90
4:16	94
5:1–10	87
5:14	95
5:17	87
5:20	90
6:1	90
6:4–5	94
7:4	109
12	93

Ephesians

1:20–23	5
1:15–23	5
3:17—18	xii
3:17–19	96
3:18–19	67, 96

Philippians

4:6–7	109
4:7	14

Colossians

1:20	88
1:27	24, 52
2:10	5
3:1–4	ix, 8, 27, 100
3:15	41, 48
3:16	34, 44

1 Timothy

2:8	14

Hebrews

1:1–4	3, 19, 21
3:1	28
3:15	95
4:14–16	4, 83
9	20
12:1–3	x
12:15	95

James

1:19–20	14

1 Peter

1–2	88

Revelation

7:10	19

Author Index

Augustine, 11–12, 13

Bediako, Kwame, 3–4
Bloesch, Donald, 55
Bridges, Matthew, 10
Buchanan, Mark, 43–44

Calvin, John, 22, 60
Cheng, Nien, 108

Dahms, John, 45

Ellul, Jacques, 19, 73

Farrow, Douglas, 21, 28, 45

Ignatius of Loyola, 56, 63–64

John of the Cross, 39, 53–54, 57, 58, 59, 66
Julian of Norwich, 58

Keener, Craig, 2–3
Kierkegaard, Soren, 38

Lin, Swee Hong, 37

Martin, Ralph, 86, 91
McAlpine, William, 47
McDowell, Josh, 12

Newbigin, Leslie, 81

Otto, Rudolf, 32

Petersen, Eugene, 100
Pieper, Joseph, 38
Plato, 38

Reynolds, Simon, 43
Ruth, Lester, 37

Scruton, Roger, 35, 36, 39
Simpson, A.B., 66

Taylor, Charles, 31–32
Teresa of Avila, 12, 53, 57, 60, 64
Tozer, A.W., 50–51, 54, 55

Webber, Robert, 35–36, 39, 47
Wesley, Charles, 10–11, 18
Wesley, John, 46
Williams, Rowan, 51, 58, 67
Wright, N.T., 101

Hymn and Song Index

Arise My Soul Arise, 10

Build Your Kingdom Here, 72

Come Thou Fount, 9, 14
Come Thou Long Expected Jesus, 18
Crown Him with Many Crowns, 10

I Know that My Redeemer Lives, 10

Jesus Thou Joy of Loving Hearts, 48, 110

O the Deep Deep Love of Jesus, 58

Once It Was the Blessing, 66
Onward Christian Soldiers, 72

Praise to the Lord, the Almighty, 14

Rejoice The Lord is King, 10–11

Spirit of God Descend Upon My Heart, 62

There's a Wideness in God's Mercy, 84
Turn Your Eyes Upon Jesus, 65

Subject Index

Abraham Lincoln, 79

Book of Common Prayer, 6–7

Caravaggio, M., 35, 106
Cheng, Nien, 107–8
Choral Evensong, 43
Church, 28, 80ff
Consolation, 109–110
Catholic Integralism, 72
Christian Nationalism, 71–72
Cross Crucifixion, 16, 19–21

Hospitality, 84

Incarnation, 16, 18–19

Lord's Supper, 19 45

Mary, 18
Messiah (Handel's), 107

New Covenant, 87

Palm Sunday, 26
Pentecost, 23–24
Preaching/Sermon/Kerygma, 44
Psalms, 100–105

Resurrection Easter, 16, 21–22

Second Coming, 24–25
Spiritual Journal, 97
Sursum Corda, 12

Willoughby, Robert, 92

www.ingramcontent.com/pod-product-compliance
Lightning Source LLC
Chambersburg PA
CBHW030903170426
43193CB00009BA/718